Introductory Note

British dance has been increasingly enriched over the years by exposure to the vast variety of forms and styles from Asia. Asia, that is, in its true geographical sense – from the Eastern Mediterranean to Japan. This selection records the visits to these shores of important companies and significant dancers who have provided not only aesthetic satisfaction but have also contributed to artistic and intellectual understanding.

The presence in the United Kingdom of many citizens who themselves, or whose parents, originated in the Indian subcontinent gives the pieces on Indian dance added dimension. Indeed, the dance of South Asia has, as it were, found a home in Britain. There are many students and scholars now working in the field of Indian dance in this country and these reviews – spanning thirty years of appreciation and constructive criticism – will, I trust, be of particular interest to them.

In Praise of the Pioneers, however, takes us back to earlier times when geniuses such as Uday Shankar and Ram Gopal initially introduced the West to the beauty and power of India's dance art.

This selection is dedicated to the pioneers and, in particular, to Anna Pavlova who pointed the way.

RM

Acknowledgements

The author and publishers would like to express their thanks to the Bharatiya Vidya Bhavan, the leading centre for Asian dance, music and culture in the United Kingdom, for its support and co-operation.

We would also like to thank *The Dancing Times* for allowing us to reproduce so many articles originially published in its pages.

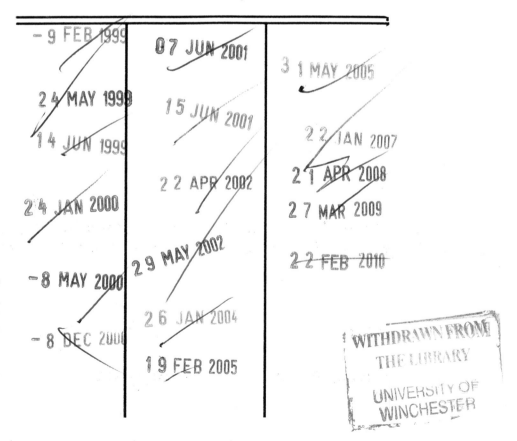

Contents

	Page
Buddha's Temptation. The Guardian. 10 Sep, 1966	**1**
The Dance and Music of Pakistan. The Dancing Times. LVII, 676, Jan 1967, pp 188-89, 195	**2-3**
Classical Dances of India. The Dancing Times. LVII, 679, Apr 1967, pp 358-359	**4-5**
Kathakali in London. The Dancing Times. LVIII, 685, Oct 1967, pp 27-29	**6-8**
Versatile Dancer. The Dancing Times. LVIII, 694, Jul 1968, p 519	**9**
Indian Dance. The Times. 30 Apr 1969	**10**
Shanta Rao. The Dancing Times. LX, 710, Nov 1969, p 87	**11**
Indian Dancers. The Dancing Times. LX, 718, Jul 1970, p 519	**12**
Gagaku. The Dancing Times. LX, 718, Jul 1970, p 519	**13**
Indian Dance in London. The Dancing Times. LXI, 722, Nov 1970, p 82	**14**
Manipuri. The Dancing Times. LXI, 724, Jan 1971, p203	**15**
Burma and India. The Dancing Times. LXI, 730, Jul 1971, p 530	**16**
India and Ceylon. The Dancing Times, LXI, 732, Sep 1971, p 654	**17**
Dervish Dancers. The Dancing Times. LXII, 736, Jan 1972, p 207	**18**
Korean Classics at The Place. The Dancing Times. LXII, 739, Apr 1972, p 373	**19**
Epics from India. The Dancing Times. LXII, 742, Jul 1972, pp 531-532	**20-21**
Kabuki. The Dancing Times. LXII, 743, Aug 1972, p 584	**22**
Beautiful Koreans. The Dancing Times. LXIII, 745, Oct 1972, p 21	**23**
Persian Delights at the Wells. The Dancing Times. LXIII, 747, Dec 1972, pp 137-139	**24-25**
North Koreans. The Dancing Times. LXIII, 751, Apr 1973, p 374	**26**
Bayanihan. The Dancing Times. LXIII, 754, Jul 1973, p 542	**27**

© 1996, Reginald Massey
Published by the NRCD

Mohini Attam. The Dancing Times. LXIV, 762, Mar 1974, p 338   **28**

Dancers from Pakistan. The Dancing Times. LXV, 778, Jul 1975, p 535   **29**

Dances from India. The Dancing Times. LXVI, 781, Oct 1975, p 27   **30**

Uday Shankar. The Times. 29 Sep 1977   **31**

The Wells of Eastern Promise. The Dancing Times. LXVIII, 805, Oct 1977, p 30   **32**

Kuchipudi Classics. The Dancing Times. LXVIII, 807, Dec 1977, p 157   **33**

Indian and Balinese dancing in London. The Dancing Times. LXVIII, 815, Aug 1978, p 655   **34**

Eastern Delights. The Dancing Times. LXXII, 864, Sept 1982, p 905   **35**

Tribute to Bharati. The Dancing Times. LXXIII, 869, Feb 1983, p 383   **36**

Balasaraswati. The Dancing Times. LXXIV, 884, May 1984, p 681   **37**

Indian Festival. The Dancing Times. LXXVIII, 925, Oct 1987, p 47   **38**

Dance Study Supplement – Asian Dance. The Dancing Times. LXXX, 955, Apr 1990, pp i–viii   **39-46**

Indonesians and Indians. The Dancing Times. LXXXI, 961, Oct 1990, pp 37-38   **47**

Indian dance in Britain. The Dancing Times. LXXXII, 989, Feb 1993, pp 452-453   **48-49**

Anandavalli. The Dancing Times. LXXXV, 1013, Feb 1995, pp 469-471   **50**

Indian Dance Captivates. The Dancing Times. LXXXV, 1020, Sep 1995, pp 1161-1163   **51-52**

Darpana Delights and Excites. The Dancing Times. LXXXVI, 1022, Nov 1995, pp 147-149   **53-54**

In Praise of the Pioneers. South Asian Dance – the British experience. Choreography and Dance. Vol 4, Part III, 1996, Harwood Academic Publishers   **55-60**

BUDDHA'S TEMPTATION

by Reginald Massey

THE holy men of this world have always, at some time or other in their careers, been tempted with the kingdoms of the earth and the pleasures of the flesh. The prince Gautama of the Sakyas was one such. He, many years before Jesus, went on a voyage of discovery so that the whys and wherefores of human existence could be adequately explained.

"The Temptation of Buddha," which was presented by the Asian Music Circle on Thursday night at the Commonwealth Institute, is a dance-drama which depicts the events of the last night before Gautama attained enlightenment.

Mara, the Evil One, danced with tremendous power by Krishna Rao, now plots to disturb Gautama's meditations. He brings on the dancing girls, his own daughters well versed in the arts of seduction, he brings in an illusory Yashodhara, Gautama's wife, who pleads with him to return to the comforts and consolations of the palace, he himself in desperation resorts to violence. But the lord is unmoved. Good prevails and evil is vanquished.

Chandrabhaga Devi's Yashodhara and Sujata are danced with lyric grace and Suresh Mahavir's Buddha is a lesson in yoga. Krishna Rao's European pupils give a good account of themselves.

The Dance and Music of Pakistan. <u>The Dancing Times</u>. LVII, 676, Jan 1967, pp 188-89, 195

2

The Dance and Music of Pakistan

by REGINALD MASSEY

The author of this article is a poet and writer on the arts of the Indian subcontinent. His book on the classical dances of the subcontinent, written in collaboration with the dancer Rina Singha, is being published later this year by Faber and Faber. The photographs are of the members of the Pakistani dance company who have been appearing at the Commonwealth Institute (when President Ayub Khan entertained the Royal Family) and elsewhere. The picture above is of the carefree peasant girls who, in the ballet Sons of the Rivers, *symbolise the happy life of the people. Below, is Rosham Ara Bokhari in a folk dance from the Sind region of West Pakistan.*

PAKISTAN, WHICH IS THE MOST POPULOUS Muslim country in the world, has for some reason not received the attention it deserves from writers on arts subjects. In 1947, the British Empire of India was partitioned into two separate sovereign states. The areas that were predominantly Hindu made up the territory of India and the areas of Muslim preponderance formed the new state of Pakistan, with its two units of East and West Pakistan separated by about a thousand miles. The cultural and ethnic differences between the two wings of this new country are extremely wide and they are held together chiefly by the bond of religion, that is, Islam.

Pakistan is less than twenty years old and therefore it is impossible to give a survey of any aspect of Pakistani life or art without discussing the Indian subcontinent as a whole. Indeed, it would be an injustice to the heritage of Pakistan to restrict the discussion to so short a period of time.

Islam does not countenance the use of music, dancing or painting as expressions of religious feeling. It insists, rather, on the pure and austere life and the performance of good works. With the passage of time, however, the simple religion of the Arabs came into contact with the sophisticated cultures of Persia and India, and the first Muslims to come to the Indian subcontinent were iconoclasts who would have no truck with any of the native Hindu arts. But later, tolerant Muslim rulers in India actively encouraged the arts, particularly the art of music. Some of the greatest musicians of the subcontinent, such as Amir Khusro and Mian Tansen, were Muslims. And this is so even today.

Schools and traditions of music were founded and these synthesised the modes and forms of Arabia, Persia and India. The basic foundation of this new style of music remained the rich store of *rāgas* (translated freely as musical modes) and the vast variety of *tāls* (time measures) already existing in India. These were added to and elaborated upon—*rāgas* such as Yemeni, for example, clearly indicate their place of origin.

The great quality that this music of the northern half of the subcontinent possessed was its ability to absorb the very best from widely differing cultures, racial groups and religions. This music flourished and reached the highest point of its development during the time of the Mughal Empire. It was known as Hindustani music to distinguish it from Karnatic music, the style native to the southern parts of the subcontinent. In India the term "Hindustani music" is still applied as such, whereas in Pakistan the term "Pakistani music" is used. Both in Pakistan and in India, the ancient schools, or *gharanas* as they are called, still exist and there are leading musicians today to whom the art has been handed down in direct line through twenty generations or more.

The classical dance style of the north of the subcontinent is called Kathak. The name originates from the word *katha*, meaning story. In ancient times, long before the Islamic influence was felt in India, the equivalent of the European bards or troubadors were the *kathaks* or story-tellers. Most of their subject matter was taken from the Rig-veda, the Mahabharata and the Ramayana. They used mime and music and later added gestures of the body and foot movements to convey their stories more vividly. This was the genesis of the Kathak dance

form.

North India has had innumerable invasions, among them that of Alexander in the fourth century B.C. Since the Greeks were themselves a highly civilised people, their cultural impact was significant and their influence on sculpture is obvious from the Grecian features of the Gandharva Buddhas. It is logical, therefore, to deduce that the dance too was probably not untouched.

Some time between the second century B.C. and the third century A.D. the Natya Shastra was written. This laid down the rules for dance, drama and music. The author is said to be one Bharata, a Brahmin, and his treatise has been the greatest single influence on the dance of the subcontinent. Bharata enumerates the various types of dance existing at the time in the different regions, examines their aims and objects, suggests appropriate music and costumes, analyses *ras* (sentiment) and *bhava* (mood) and indicates how these are to be conveyed by the artist. He maintains that drama must be didactic and also "give courage, amusement, as well as counsel". Now, as drama, dance and music formed an equally important part of a composite programme, what he said of drama applied to dance and vice versa.

The Hindus used these arts for religious as well as secular purposes and each temple had its *devadasis* or female attendants of the gods who were in effect temple dancers and courtesans. This was perhaps an additional reason for the Muslim aversion to the use of dancing for religious purposes. Nevertheless, they encouraged dancing in the courts and during the Mughal period Kathak became a sophisticated art form for the delectation of the connoisseur. The repertoire of Kathak was enriched and considerably expanded to include secular subject matter with a Muslim background.

With the decline of the Mughal Empire the patronage of Kathak was largely taken over by the Rajahs and Nawabs. It was they who kept Kathak alive for over two centuries. The greatest patron of modern times was Wajid Ali Shah, the last Nawab of Avadh, in whose court the first dance-drama in Urdu verse, entitled "Inder Sabha" or "The Court of Indra", was performed.

Kathak, therefore, is the common heritage of Pakistan and India, a fact which could be more widely appreciated.

In early December, the talented Pakistani choreographer Mehr Nigar Hosain presented her ballet *Sons of the Rivers* in London. It was an interesting experiment in that she is trying to forge her own individual idiom. Her technique is based only partly on Kathak and incorporates to a large extent both folk and expressionistic dance movements. From this it is clear that she is attempting to create a ballet style which, while retaining its essentially Pakistani character, will be easily appreciated not only by those who are familiar with the classical dances of the subcontinent but also

Two Pakistani artists in a peasant dance about the troubles of a nomad snake-charmer.

by the average theatregoer in any part of the world.

The ballet tells the story of the coming of the Greeks to the Punjab—the land of the Five Rivers—and the peoples' struggle for freedom. The costumes were authentic and the décor excellent, although the accompanying orchestrated music could well have been somewhat less influenced by the West. The dancers presented a clarity of line that does credit to their training but this was sometimes confused by the restricted stage conditions of the Commonwealth Institute.

There were musical interludes, notably by Nathu Khan on the Sarangi (a stringed instrument played with a bow), Alla Ditta Khan on the Tabla (a pair of drums), and Khamisoo Khan on the Alghoza (a double flute). They played with fluency and feeling and a larger contribution from them

In the ballet Sons of the Rivers, *the peasants rise in revolt.*

would have been most welcome.

Also presented were some folk dances from both East and West Pakistan which were closely related to the daily life of the people. The dances from East Pakistan showed a distinct affinity with the classical dances of Manipur.

The programme notes were inadequate and the date of Alexander's invasion was incorrect. It was perhaps by an unfortunate error that the Greeks wore green, the national colour of Pakistan.

This was the first visit of Pakistani dances and musicians to Britain and we hope to see more of them in the future.

4

Classical Dances of India. The Dancing Times. LVII, 679, Apr 1967, pp 358-359

THE EARLIEST CIVILIZATION OF THE INDIAN subcontinent grew in the Indus valley and is dated at about 6000 B.C. Among the many interesting finds in the cities of Mohenjo Daro and Harappa is an exquisite statuette of a dancing girl. Not surprisingly, however, we know almost nothing about the form or technique of her dance.

The Aryans came to India around 2000 B.C. and it was they who moulded the religious, social and economic structure of the subcontinent. The *shastras* or books of learning were set down and the epics, the Ramayana and the Mahabharata, were composed. The arts were studied, analysed, and codified into a vast corpus of knowledge which amazes the present-day critic by its scientific approach, its psychological insight and above all, by the genuine concern of the ancients for the cultural life of the people.

It is obviously impossible within the space available here to do justice to all the theories upon which Indian dancing is based. The labyrinthine ways of the Brahminical mind defy simplification. However, familiarity with at least a few of the principles involved can only add to the understanding and appreciation of the art.

The *shastra* on dance, drama, and music, known as the Bharata Natya Shastra, is believed to have been written by a sage named Bharata who lived some time between the second century B.C. and the third century A.D. The discovery of the manuscript of this work was made by Hall in the latter half of the last century, but it was not until 1950 that the first English translation by Ghosh appeared.

The Bharata Natya Shastra classifies dance as either *tandav* or *lasya*. *Tandav* is that which expresses actions and feelings with strength and vigour. It is essentially a masculine dance, the dance of the god Shiva who is the symbol of virility and procreation. *Lasya,* by contrast, is the dance of Parvati, Shiva's consort, and emphasizes all the feminine feelings and attributes.

The *shastra* also lays down that there are three aspects of the dance. The first is *natya* which may be described as its dramatic aspect, " a mimicry of the exploits of gods, asuras (demons), kings, as well as of householders." The second is *nritta* which comprises the rhythmic and decorative movements of the body in dance. The third and perhaps the most important aspect is *nritya* whose function is to suggest *ras* (emotional state or sentiment) and *bhava* (mood). An exhaustive analysis explains how this is to be achieved, and covers everything from costume and music, to gestures for almost every part of the body. There are, for example, seven movements for the eyeballs and nine for the neck.

The emotional states or sentiments known as *rasas* are nine in number, namely, love, humour, pathos, anger, heroism, terror, disgust, wonder, and

Classical Dances of India

by REGINALD MASSEY

Photographs by Marc Alexander

Above, Indrani in the sculpturesque Odissi dance. Opposite top, the liquid movements of Manipuri interpreted by the Jhaveri sisters; centre, the triumphant hero, Shekaran in Kathakali; below, Kathak in Mughal costume, Uma Sharma and Devilal caught at the end of a sequence.

serenity. The dancer has to master all the arts of expression so as to be able to convey these *rasas* as effectively as possible.

A combination of various gestures, which together form a single unit of dance, is called a *karana*. Indian dancers have been inspired for hundreds of years by the 108 *karanas* carved into the four gateways

of the temple at Chidambaram in South India. Evidently the early dance theorists wished to supplement the written word by illustrations in a durable form.

There are four main classical dances in India and each of these has subsidiary forms with their own traditions which reflect ethnic, religious, and political influences.

In the north there exists the Kathak dance which had its genesis with the *kathaks* or storytellers who disseminated moral and religious instruction in the form of *kathas* or stories. With the passage of time they added music, mime, and dance to their repertoire. Later, when the rulers were Muslims, Kathak was brought into the court and became more secular in the process.

In the north-east the chief dance is Manipuri. It is a perfect blending of music and movement in soft and gentle patterns reflecting the life and religion of the people of that area.

Kathakali is the dance-drama indigenous to the south-west of India within the area of what is now the state of Kerala. This is a *tandav* dance which depicts the exploits of legendary heroes, the villainies of demons, the benignity of the gods, and the treacheries of ogresses. It has a comprehensive vocabulary of gestures of the hands and face, and particularly of the movements of the eyes.

The south-east is the home of Bharata Natyam which is a solo dance and originated with the *devadasis* or female temple dancers who attended upon the gods in the temples. An important feature of this dance is the interpretation of poems in praise of various deities.

Two dances that have been rediscovered of late are Kuchipudi and Odissi. The former was originally a dance-drama for men, but is known today chiefly through extracts performed by solo dancers in the course of their programmes. The latter was a solo dance preserved in the remote temples of Orissa and performed there by temple dancers. It is a most interesting dance as it combines elements from both South and North India, for whereas the dance movements show an affinity with Bharata Natyam, the accompanying music is north Indian in character.

One who has done much to revive interest in this beautiful dance is Indrani, who with her company had a three week season (from January 23rd to February 11th) at the Scala Theatre. Most of her contributions to the programmes were in Odissi. The ease and fluidity with which one sculpturesque pose melted into another in this most feminine of dances was captivating. The infectious warmth of her personality immediately conveyed itself to her audience. Her Kuchipudi piece *Mohini Avatara* related how the gods and the demons together churned the ocean in order to obtain the nectar of immortality. However once this had been done the gods were reluctant to share it with the demons.

observed imitation of nature. The *Peacock Dance* captured exactly the behaviour of this vain and fastidious bird. The graphic portrayal of the Mahabharata story of the elephant and the crocodile gave to it the colour of a parable. The confident swaying gait of the elephant demonstrated his majesty as he surveyed the forest of which he was master, but the warted crocodile, denizen of the slime, lay in wait. Without warning he struck. One moment Shekaran was the elephant struggling for his life, the next he was the vicious saurian who knew he could not lose by the water's edge. Humbled at last, because he realised he was losing the fight, the elephant sued to Vishnu the Preserver for aid. His prayers were answered and the lesson was learnt. Shekaran's dancing displayed the ability of Kathakali to evoke dramatically suspense, pity, and fear.

Unfortunately, London has not yet had the opportunity of seeing and assessing a full Kathakali company. A group was to have come for the first Commonwealth Arts Festival in 1965, but was prevented from doing so because of the tragic conflict between the two countries of the subcontinent.

The accompanying music was provided by a group of talented musicians many of whom had to play in the different styles appropriate to the dances. Their leader was Parashar Desai, and the other players were Arun Kumar, Seshadri, Srinivasa Murthy, Suryanarayan, Valvant Rai Verma, Senayaima Singh, C. Hasmukh and Sukanya.

The presentation as a whole was extremely enjoyable, providing as it did the opportunity of seeing several of India's dances and of observing their similarities and differences. It is rare indeed to see so many excellent artistes performing in the same programme. Birendra Shankar is to be congratulated on bringing them to this country.

The god Vishnu therefore took on the form of the beautiful seductress Mohini. This lovely vision distracted the attention of the demons with blandishments and meanwhile ladled out the nectar to the gods. Indrani danced the story with obvious enjoyment and the clarity of her expression made it easy to follow the episode from beginning to end. The *Tillana* of Bharata Natyam is a dance with no specific meaning, in which rhythmic variations are given full play in combination with decorative movements of the body. If anything, it expresses the dancer's sheer joy in her art. Indrani's *Tillana* did just this.

The four Jhaveri sisters are well known exponents of Manipuri but on this occasion because one of them was unable to come they were joined by Kalavati Singh. The delicate grace of their gentle movements was enhanced by the sparkle of their costumes. Their programme was varied and particularly attractive were the *Holika Kreeda*, which celebrated the coming of spring and the *Khanduk Khel*, a sequence about the young god Krishna playing a ball game. Guru Bipin Singh's choreography made good use of the stage space, but nevertheless some of the dances might, with advantage, have been abbreviated slightly.

Kathak was well represented by Uma Sharma. This young dancer has great vivacity and a wide range of expression. Her *Khandita Nayika* conveyed eloquently the careful preparations of a maiden for the love tryst, her anxiety and rising impatience when her lord is late, her angry rejection of him when he finally does arrive, and her remorse when he has left. The accuracy of her incredibly fast pirouettes and footwork showed her grasp of *tal* (time measure) and it is a pity that during these passages her arm movements became somewhat sketchy. The competitive duets, *Jugal Bandi*, with Devilal generated excitement and were danced with panache and style.

Shekaran was the sole representative of the Kathakali dance-drama which has such distinctive make up and costumes. He therefore had to restrict himself to brief character sketches and short pure dance pieces. In spite of this he was able to show the power of Kathakali and its well

Kathakali in London. <u>The Dancing Times</u>. LVIII, 685, Oct 1967, pp 27-29

Kathakali in London

by
REGINALD MASSEY

drawings by
ABU

The drawing at the head of the page shows the two types of drums used in Kathakali—the Maddalam (left) and the Chenda.

KATHAKALI IS THE DANCE DRAMA OF Kerala, one of the smallest states of the Indian Union. The state faces the Arabian Sea and occupies the western strip of the peninsula right down to Cape Comorin.

The indigenous people of Kerala were of the Dravidian race but much later the Aryan Brahmins from the north also settled in the country. Kathakali, as we know it today, is the result of the marriage between the pre-Aryan dances and the later ones introduced under Brahmin influence. With the coming of the Brahmins the Nayar warrior caste, who were half Aryan and half Dravidian, came into being. They formed the soldiery of the state. Even when the need for them to fight had disappeared however, they continued to practise their martial dances and their highly scientific physical exercises in their gymnasia. It is these exercises which form a vital part of Kathakali training to this day. This is evident not only in the obviously masculine form of their dance but also in the basic stance for Kathakali—knees bent and held wide apart to allow freedom of movement in any direction.

The immediate predecessor of Kathakali was a dance drama about the god Krishna written in 1650 by the Zamorin (ruler) of Calicut. The fame of this *Krishna Attam* reached his neighbour the Raja of Kottarakkara, who expressed a desire to see it. The Zamorin's contemptuous reply was that no one in Kottarakkara was cultured enough to appreciate its subtleties. Consequently the offended Raja, with the help of the Raja of Kottayam, wrote one of his own dealing with the life of the epic hero Rama. Unlike the Zamorin's play however, which was in Sanskrit, his was in the regional language and so could be understood by all. *Raman Attam*, therefore, quickly became popular and was soon augmented by dance dramas from the whole of the Ramayana, the Mahabharata, and other sacred texts. The name of this dance form had now to be changed to Kathakali, story-play, which was more appropriate to the wider thematic range.

Kathakali flourished under the patronage of the princes of Kerala, who not only supported it but wrote for it and even performed it themselves. It reached its peak during the eighteenth century but by the mid-nineteenth century, when the power of the rajas had weakened and the atmosphere of foreign rule was unsympathetic to the Indian arts, the decline had set in. The revival is due almost entirely to the poet Vallathol who, in 1930, finally succeeded in establishing the Kerala Kala Mandalam, and brought to it the finest teachers of Kathakali then alive. It is now one of the leading dance institutes of India.

Kathakali is an art at once of fantasy and of realism. The whole text is sung by musicians and the dancer-actors never actually speak, yet this is soon forgotten because of the rich variety of their gestural language. All Kathakali stories are about gods, heroes and demons. The extravagance of its costumes, the symbolism of its make-up both in colour and form, and its stylised action lift the drama to a superhuman level and help to suspend disbelief; at the same time its accurate observation of life, its meticulous attention to detail, its extremely correct sense of proportion, lend it an air of familiarity so that the total effect, in spite of the appearance of fantasy, is one of uncanny realism.

The company of the Kerala Kala Mandalam, in London for the first time, presented three programmes in a season at the Saville Theatre in August. All were, of necessity, greatly shortened since each dance drama lasts from evening through into dawn the next day.

Nala Charita was the romantic story of King Nala and Damayanti, the beautiful princess whom even the gods covet. It tells of their love for each other and the conduct of their courtship through the mediation of a golden swan. So true is their love that in the end the gods retire from the competition for her hand, and leave the lovers free to marry.

The episode chosen from the Ramayana was about the abduction of Sita. The prince Rama, his wife Sita, and his brother Lakshmana are living exiled in the forest. The villain of the piece is Ravana, the demon king of Ceylon, who has vowed to avenge his sister Surpanakha, disfigured by Lakshmana because she persisted in trying to seduce him and Rama. Ravana and his uncle Maricha hatch a plot. Maricha appears as a beautiful deer and lures Rama away. When Rama shoots the deer, Maricha imitates his voice and calls for help. Sita, convinced that Rama is in trouble, forces Lakshmana to go to his

Krishna's final dance, Dhanasi, at the end of the Mahabharata (photograph by Marc Alexander).

Rama, hero of the Ramayana.

brother's assistance. Ravana meanwhile carries off Sita in his flying chariot. They meet Jatayu the king of the birds, who tries to stop Ravana, fights him, and is mortally wounded. Rama and Lakshmana see Jatayu on their way back and learn of the abduction of Sita. In order to avenge this crime, Rama forms an alliance with Sugriva, the monkey, who is at war with his own brother Bali. Emboldened by his alliance with the mighty Rama, Sugriva challenges Bali to a personal combat. The wicked Bali is winning when Rama shoots him in order that justice might be done. Rama is now ready to go in quest of his wife and rescue her.

Vasudevan Nayar's performance as Jatayu was most impressive. The brave bird, tricked by the demonic Ravana, shorn of his pinions, excited pity from even the most stone-hearted in the audience as it lay quivering and panting out its last breath.

Ramankutty Nayar, an eminent teacher and leader of the company, danced Ravana with Lucifer-like grandeur.

The contest between Bali and Sugriva, danced by Krishnan Nayar and Vasu Namboodiri, was a characteristic example of observation from life. They behaved exactly as monkeys do when they fight but were, at the same time, reminiscent of humans, revealing in this way the animal in human nature and the human element in animals, with more than a few touches of humour. Indeed, there was a lot of humour in the stories, humour which needed no explanation and came always from the villains, thus exposing evil to ridicule by provoking laughter at the evil-doers.

Noteworthy among the musicians were the drummers, particularly Kesavan who played the *chenda* (upright drum) most eloquently. With immobile face, he now provided imaginative sound effects, now

thundered out turmoil, now produced the gentlest of taps to emphasize the silence.

The Mahabharata opened with the dice game in which Yudhistira the eldest of the Pandava brothers loses his possessions, his four brothers, the wife they have in common, and himself to Sakuni the wily uncle of his cousins the Kauravas. Sakuni had won with unerring accuracy by the simple expedient of using loaded dice. Dushasana, the swaggering Kaurava bully insults Draupadi, the Pandavas' wife, and attempts to disrobe her in open court. In this scene Sivaraman's Draupadi (all female parts are played by men in Kathakali) was superb. With trembling lip and reproachful eye, shouted at and taunted

because her husbands could not help her, she was utterly dejected. Yet after the final insult she visibly summoned up all her courage, bit back her tears and, woman though she was, went boldly up to Dushasana and flung a curse in his face. One day her husband Bhima would disembowel him and, until it could be dressed with his blood, she would not bind up her hair. The part was so beautifully performed that it took a conscious effort to remember there was a man behind the make-up. Sivaraman built up her character until she was truly a woman injured, and with a righteous cause.

The banished Pandavas, disguised as servants, work in a palace. Kichaka, the vain and lecherous brother of the queen, tries to seduce Draupadi—a scene acted by Krishnan Nayar with great relish and humour—but by employing a ruse Bhima kills him.

The thirteen years of the Pandavas' banishment over, they ask the god Krishna to negotiate for them with the Kauravas. The Kauravas refuse; they will give the Pandavas not so much as a pinhead of land.

It is now war to the bitter end.

The opposing armies face each other on the battlefield of Kurukshetra. On his chariot Arjuna, the third brother, leads the Pandavas, with Krishna himself as his charioteer. Seeing the Kaurava army, Arjuna is filled with dismay. How can he fight his own uncles, his cousins, his old teachers, his good friends, and himself bring about their slaughter? It would be sinful. He cannot fight them.

Krishna now delivers his message—the Bhagavad Gita, or the Song Divine. Arjuna must do his duty no matter what the cost in blood and tears. It is only through duty done without flinching, that Divine Order will be established.

The Pandavas (photograph by Maria Austria).

Draupadi, wife of the five Pandava brothers.

The armies do battle and the Kauravas are vanquished. Like Macduff searching out Macbeth, Bhima goes to confront his wife's humiliator. Driven to a frenzy by Dushasana's taunts, Bhima takes on the form of a man-lion. At last after a long struggle, Dushasana is overcome and Bhima proceeds to disembowel him. The horrifying realism of the acting is heightened when Bhima stares wildly at his blood-soaked hands and brings up between his teeth strings of gory entrails, as Dushasana writhes and gasps his life away. Bhima then fulfils his pledge and binds Draupadi's hair with his dripping hands.

Still in a rage, he sees Krishna and falls at the god's feet. Krishna blesses him and purges him of his fury. Justice is done and the wrong avenged. As is usual in Kathakali, the action ends on a calm note with a benediction.

This last is particularly important in a dance drama like the Mahabharata where almost every human emotion is laid bare and where the climax draws the audience to a high emotional pitch. Nerves are tautened, and the mental balance is disturbed. The *dhanasi* or final blessing really does prove the Indian theory that not only must the artist evoke a particular sentiment in himself and be seen to evoke it, but that he must also call it forth in his audience. To be able to evoke tranquility immediately after the spectators have been tuned up to such terrible violence, is a measure of the power of Kathakali.

The catharsis is complete, even though achieved by the antithesis of Aristotle's precepts. This is, perhaps, one of the fascinations of Kathakali.

Versatile Dancer. <u>The Dancing Times</u>. LVIII, 694, Jul 1968, p 519

In India it is only comparatively recently that classical dancers and musicians have attempted to learn and practise styles other than their own. Of course, when they do this they risk their reputations and are, more often than not, accused of insincerity and currying favour with wider audiences. No such charge can be levelled against Ritha Devi who performed at the Commonwealth Institute on June 6th, 7th and 8th.

Ritha Devi danced a number of styles with the major exceptions of Kathak, the classical dance of North India, and Manipuri, the dance of North-East India. Ritha Devi does not dance Kathak, but it is a pity she omitted Manipuri for she is a Bengali and comes from a family that has done much to put Manipuri on the dance map of India. However, her repertoire, consisting of items from eastern and southern India, was most pleasing and satisfying.

The rarely performed *Navasandhi*, a prayer to Brahma the Creator and eight other deities, was danced with beauty and devotion and left one with the thought that if more prayers were as appealing many more people would be praying today. The plainsong-like chant that accompanied the dance gave it " meaning " in the Occidental sense. The other Kuchipudi item was the charming *Krishna Shabdam* in which a coquettish milkmaid tries to entice the god with human blandishments.

The virility and power of Kathakali was seen in London last year. It is therefore no wonder that this dance-drama is the preserve of men, even the female parts being taken by male dancers. Ritha Devi nevertheless took one episode from Kathakali and performed it as a solo item. This was *Putana-Moksham* in which the demoness Putana, disguised as the beautiful Lalita, comes to poison the infant god Krishna. She smears poison on her breasts and suckles the child. Soon, she thinks, the child will be dead. But it is her life that is drained away from her. A difficult piece danced well, but Ritha Devi did not somehow light that vital spark which could have burst into flame. Also, a minor but significant point: the doll used to represent the infant was fair faced. Krishna was dark-complexioned, Le Dieu Bleu, the Dark One.

Odissi, the temple dance of eastern India, was well represented by the stories of Draupadi and Ahalya, the suffering heroines of Hindu mythology. They are symbols of womanhood; ill-used by men and gods and ground down by evil circumstance. Draupadi and Ahalya are, in fact, still with us in the world today. Ritha Devi danced Draupadi with dramatic power, a sadly neglected aspect of the graceful and essentially liquid Odissi style, but it was as Ahalya that one saw her art at its best.

Ritha Devi's introductions were useful guides for the dances which followed. Other Indian artists could well do the same. Her accompanists, Sri Kunjitham, Sri Santhanam, and Sri Jayakar, provided excellent vocal and instrumental music and I must not forget to mention the valiant little Rahul who rendered valuable service on the drone instrument.

REGINALD MASSEY

Versatile Dancer

Ritha Devi in Odissi, the dance style in which she particularly excelled (photograph by Marc Alexander).

Indian Dance. <u>The Times</u>. 30 Apr 1969

Indian dance

The classical dance of the northern part of the India-Pakistan sub-continent is not often seen in London and it was praiseworthy of the Society of Indian Music to present a Kathak programme at the V. & A. last night. The danseuse they chose was Sitara, an artist of virtuosity and fire who is fully qualified to project the two great influences that have shaped this style, the Hindu and the Muslim.

The first half of the night's offering was secular: lightning pirouettes, tantalizing syllables first recited and then repeated on the tabla and the ankle-bells, cross-rhythms, the excitement generated by the competition of dancer and percussionist. All this constituted the *nritta*, the pure dance.

After the interval drama, poetry and pathos were introduced. The first *thumri*, danced poem, by Binda Din was disappointing. The coyness inherent in the lyric was strangely lacking. The second *thumri* made up for this more than adequately through the splendid use of mime and gesture. There before our eyes was Radha herself imploring the God Krishna with tenderness and pathos —but he, the incarnation of Vishnu, had heard the call to action and would not be persuaded.

Latif Ahmed Khan on the tabla and Fida Hussain, harmonium, played with panache and an un-erring ear.

R.M.

Shanta Rao

Superb Kathakali

GOOD DANCERS OFTEN MAKE COMPETENT choreographers: but is it always so? The question assumes added significance in an Indian context where acceptance comes with age and imprimaturs are issued only by the *gurus*—a worthwhile practise, perhaps, if the purity of a tradition is to be kept intact and preserved. These are the thoughts that exercised my mind when I saw Shanta Rao present a programme of dances at the Royal Festival Hall on September 22nd. She had just appeared at the Windsor Festival, was touring the continent after London, and was in excellent form. One therefore expected dancing of the highest order, dancing that would transport the audience to a plane far removed from the prosaic and the earthbound. This effect was not achieved during the first half of the evening and the causative factor was not, I am sure, the quality and character of Shanta Rao's execution but rather the poverty of her choreographic invention.

The " Bhama Nrityam " items, Shanta Rao's personal innovations, even though based on a traditional school, were by and large disappointing. The gestures were repetitive, the arms especially most inelegantly poised and the tempi painfully unvaried. The line was always being broken and fragmented by some quite unnecessary and invalid movements. The visual images therefore blurred and dissolved before an impact was registered and this is unpardonable in south Indian dancing whose hallmark is a sculpturesque clarity. Something, however, was redeemed by sheer expertise and virtuosity. The legend of Rukmini's love for Krishna was danced with pathos and showed Shanta Rao's fine acting talent. The second Krishna theme used many *mudras,* hand gestures, to good effect although the circus act of dancing on a salver—brilliant and clever as it was—left me cold.

After the interval, the pieces from the Kathakali dance-drama of south-west India were consistently well portrayed. There was now a certain sense of richness and magic on the stage and this permeated the atmosphere. She, the dancer, bridged the gulf between the mortal and the immortal and we, the audience, willingly suspended disbelief. The artist was now in her element, at one with the true and the traditional; this was Shanta Rao herself again. And the musicians, especially Mrs. K. V. Ratnam, provided able support.

BBC-2 is preparing a television documentary on Shanta Rao's visit; one awaits the broadcast with interest.

REGINALD MASSEY

Indian Dancers. The Dancing Times. LX, 718, Jul 1970, p 519

Indian Dancers

by

REGINALD MASSEY

IT IS AN EXTREMELY DIFFICULT TASK FOR ANY one dancer to give a satisfying account of four dance styles in a single evening. Indeed, I would have thought it quite impossible had I not seen Ritha Devi at the Victoria and Albert Museum on April 24th when she offered a marvellously well-edited programme. The *Mahasati Tara* legend, danced in the Odissi style of Orissa State, told of Tara's misfortunes at the hands of Rama and how the god-king finally made amends. The power and the pathos of the characters was superbly delineated and Ritha Devi demonstrated the dramatic and *tandav,* masculine, aspects of this essentially lyrical style. The subject has

not been treated by dancers for about a century and it is to Ritha Devi's credit that she brought it back to life with such telling force and poignancy. Also in Odissi was the exquisite *Konaraka Kala,* choreographed by the dancer herself and inspired by the sculptures of the Sun temple at Konarak, which depicted the eight types of *nayikas,* or classical heroines. Ritha Devi's form, line and time sense were as perfect as humanly possible.

The Shiva-Parvati dance in the Kuchipudi style of the State of Andhra was somewhat disappointing for the incorrect lighting, later rectified, combined with the messy costume to kill the vital element of contrast when the dancer's right side is the powerful god Shiva and her left side is Parvati, his consort. Apparently, some inconsiderate members of the audience had pushed about the two spotlights on either side of the hall. However, *Patim Dehi,* in Kerala State's Mohini Attam style, which came a little later set the balance right with mimetic expression and pure dance of the highest quality. It related the events which had led to Draupadi's polyandry with the five Pandava brothers in a succession of brilliantly drawn cameos. This too, was choreographed by Ritha Devi and one was made aware of her considerable talents in that direction.

The Bharata Natyam *tillana,* from Tamil Nadu State, was cleanly executed with neat pirouettes and instantaneous stillnesses. It had a controlled vivacity that never became excessive—which, incidentally, many dancers are prone to do in this dance of swift movement and strong rhythms. The last item, Kurathy, was a folk dance based upon the free use of Bharata Natyam techniques and although it was well danced, I felt its earthiness out of place in the elevated atmosphere especially as it closely followed the very moving *Mahasati Tara.* Fortunately this anti-climax was sensibly avoided in the second night's programme.

In Ritha Devi her country has an excellent cultural ambassador.

* * *

TWO DANCERS LIVING IN LONDON PRESENTED their programmes in early May: Balasundari, from Ceylon, at the Commonwealth Institute on the 2nd and 8th and Kama Dev, from South India, at the Round House on the 5th. Many of Balasundari's English pupils appeared with her and noteworthy were Mrinalini who interpreted a *pada,* love lyric, through the use of expressionistic movement involving the face, eyes and hands and Phyllis Selwyn who gave a good account of the *nritta,* pure dance, pieces. The charming Balasundari's main contribution was a *varnam,* a complex item which alternates between *nritta* and *nritya,* expression, and where the melody is rendered to the words of the song as well as to *swaras* or sol-fa syllables. There could have been more of her since some of the pupils were not quite up to scratch and to present them prematurely was most unfortunate. The peculiar liquidity

and mobility of Indian dance is not beyond the grasp of Occidentals; I have seen numerous instances of this in the past. What is required is time and patience. To rush art is to destroy it.

The young Kama Dev, who started his career with Ram Gopal, has specialised in the Kuchipudi style of Andhra Pradesh. With the presence and profile of a god he can change a symbolic myth of the past into the living reality of today; the *Dasavataamul,* showing the ten incarnations of Vishnu the Preserver, being a good example. Kama Dev's *nritya* beautifully imaged the avatars through the evolutionary ladder from fish to mighty horseman. However, it was the sparkling footwork and excellent acting in a dance about the youthful Krishna that transformed the evening. Kama Dev became, in effect, the Dark One by the banks of the Yamuna enlivening the atmosphere with a rich and strange romance. He is a dancer worth watching.

—

Gagaku. <u>The Dancing Times</u>. LX, 718, Jul 1970, p 519

Gagaku

THE PECULIAR GENIUS OF THE JAPANESE people to import, adapt, develop and completely "Nipponize" foreign influences was seen at its best at the Royal Albert Hall on May 28th when their Imperial Court artists appeared in this country for the very first time. The programme consisted of dance and musical items inspired from Chinese, Indian, Korean and Mongolian sources apart from one of purely Japanese origin. Yet what we saw was unmistakably Japanese in idiom, atmosphere and feeling, distilled as it was through a thousand years of *gagaku* tradition.

Gagaku is the art of the abstract; the inessentials have been stripped away and the onlooker is confronted with what Hopkins called "inscape". The costumes, however, are vastly elaborate and courtly and the movements have the slow majestic splendour which can only come after years of training and which, to my mind, so magnificently states the dignity of the artist. There was the dancer-actor Togi Shintaro resplendent in the white robe of a ninth century Imperial Guard holding, as it were, the mirror up to life and reminding us that we see truth merely through a glass darkly, while in the background the solemn chant of the Zen-like poem told of benevolence and compassion. And later, as the heroic Prince of Lan-ling complete with menacing mask, he routed his enemies with a stylised prowess so typical of the brave days of old when war was honourable because it was fought according to the strictest codes of conduct. In both these solos Togi Shintaro used the few steps, the slight dips and the controlled thrusts to the limits of their expressiveness.

The English Bach Festival who presented these dancers in association with the Japan Cultural Society and the Embassy of Japan are to be congratulated for giving us the opportunity of a unique experience.

REGINALD MASSEY

14

Indian Dance in London. <u>The Dancing Times</u>. LXI, 722, Nov 1970, p 82

Indian Dance in London

Events Seen

THERE HAS BEEN MUCH INDIAN DANCE IN London in recent weeks. Uma Sharma, a leading female exponent of the north Indian Kathak style, danced in four programmes on the South Bank as part of a whole festival of Indian music and dance. On the morning of September 20th at the Queen Elizabeth Hall she started with a salutation to Saraswati, the goddess of the fine arts, and then gave a delectable piece from the Radha-Krishna repertoire. The singer accompanying her was the great Girija Devi and together they transported the eternal lovers, one human and the other divine, from the banks of the Yamuna in the Braj country of north India to the banks of the Thames in metropolitan London. That night in the same hall the Radha-Krishna theme was taken up again: with dramatic power Uma Sharma acted out the desolation and anguish of the devotee whose Lord will not come to her. Her considerable talent as an actress evoked deep feeling and sympathy and once again brought home the lesson that the artist does indeed speak an international language. Miss Sharma also possesses a good singing voice and one had a fine example of it on the next night when she rendered an exquisite *ghazal*, a lyric poem in the Urdu language, set to music. After singing a verse she would translate it into gesture and mime and punctuate the narration with pure dance movement—setting and polishing the gem as it were. For this item she wore the beautiful costume of

the Mughal court which suits Kathak dancing so admirably.

At the Royal Festival Hall on September 23rd items from the Hindu and Muslim heritage of Kathak were danced. The *Kaliya Mardana Gath* vividly depicted the subduing of the serpent Kaliya by the god Krishna and the Muslim *Court Dance* defined the subtlest shades of emotion on the one hand and gave a fiery display of rhythm and percussion on the other. If this is a foretaste of the good things to come then I can only wish Birendra Shankar, the director, and his Sanskritik Centre the very best for the future.

Vija Vetra, Latvian by birth, has studied in India and now has a dance centre in New York. Miss Vetra is working on a significant conception: she is creating Indian-inspired religious dances based on the universal truths and performing them in churches. At St. Martin-in-the-Fields on September 13th she gave some examples of her creations in which she was ably assisted by the readings of the Rev. John Kirkham. How effectively they " married " the Jewish-Christian St. Paul to the Indian poet Tagore! Later, the dance interpretations of Bach's *Jesu mein Freund*, *Jesu joy of Man's Desiring* and *Toccata in D Minor*, would have moved the most hardened cynic.

On September 16th Vija Vetra appeared at the Commonwealth Institute. The south Indian Bharata Natyam item for the Tagore poem, danced to north Indian music, was a sample of disastrous integration whereas the *Dance of Lights* was showy but nonetheless charming. However, Miss Vetra's lissom beauty was seen to best advantage in the *Tillana*, an item consisting of poses from the south Indian temple sculptures interspersed with rhythmic patterns, and her short talk was marked by a touching sincerity.

I am always sceptical about child prodigies and I had similar feelings when I went to the Victoria and Albert Museum Theatre on September 17th to see Ram Gopal introduce the thirteen-year-old Anandavalli from Ceylon. My scepticism was soon dispelled for, judged by any standards, Anandavalli is a brilliant dancer. I cannot imagine what she will be like in five years time; that is, if she is not spoilt by this early success. The dancing and acting in the elaborate *Varnam* which described eight legendary Hindu heroines had passion remarkable in one so young. The dance composition was by Anandavalli's *guru*, Lakshmana of Madras, the words were by her brother Anandakumar and the translation was by Linga, her mother: a rare combination of talents. With the pure dance *Jatiswaram* I was not so happy for although Anandavalli has a faultless sense of time measures she is unable to hold some of the poses she attempts. In fact, she tends to be too ambitious in these. Greater discipline,

A South Indian Bharata Natyam pose by Vija Vetra.

body control, and muscular development must be acquired before these difficult poses can be made to look beautiful. Anandavalli still has a great deal to learn but I have no doubt that she will go very far.

In quick conclusion: Surya Kumari, who lives and teaches in London, gave two performances at the Commonwealth Institute on October 7th and 10th in which she was assisted by Keshav Sathe on the *tabla* (a pair of north Indian drums), and at the Avatar Music Room, Kensington, on September 10th S. M. Shah played some of his interesting recordings of folk dance music from East and West Pakistan.

REGINALD MASSEY

Uma Sharma, in Mughal costume, executes a pirouette in the Kathak style of North India.

Manipuri. The Dancing Times. LXI, 724, Jan 1971, p 203

Manipuri

The dancers on the right perform one of their traditional dance dramas; the girl wears the typical bell shaped skirt.

IN THE NORTH-EASTERN CORNER OF INDIA, where the Himalayas loop southward towards the sea, lies the picturesque valley of Manipur. This is the home of the Meities, a people of slight build with slanting eyes. The Meities are a sensitive, artistic race and dance has always occupied a central position in the pattern of their daily lives. *Jagoi*, dance, was so important that the king himself headed the *Palaloisang*, dancers' guild, and had therefore to be a trained and accomplished dancer. The *Palaloisang* is even today an active body and Manipuri dance has, over the years, gained new devotees in other parts of India.

For four days, November 16th to 19th, the Triveni Dance Company appeared at the Commonwealth Institute and presented an interesting cross section of the Manipuri style. The *Vasant Ras* depicted the Festival of Colours in the Spring, the main characters being Radha and Krishna. Pretty, pretty, one would say: but then the *Ras* is just that. No great emotions here, only movements of pure joy and Arcadian bliss. More masculine were the Spear Dance and the *Pung Cholom*, a thundering, roistering drum dance, in which the leaps and the swirling on the knees had a distinct Red Army look. However, nearer the spirit of Manipuri was the ancient *Lai Haroba*, based on Meitie concepts of cosmology, and *Arjuna-Chitrangada*, a dance contest between the hero, Arjuna, and the princess, Chitrangada.

The ballet *Lei-Mun*, the Discarded Flower, told of a village chief's daughter who married a god. The lovers are happy in their heavenly abode but the villagers begin to miss the beautiful girl who was popular with one and all. So they stage a mock funeral; the girl's curiosity is aroused and she begs her husband to allow her to see what is happening. The god permits her to visit her people but warns that she must not partake of human food lest she become mortal again. The villagers—innocent of this injunction—prepare a feast to welcome the visitor and insist that she join in the festivities and eat with them. She, Eve-like, breaks the command-

ment. The god sweeps away the villagers for their part in the affair and returns to heaven. The heroine, now human again, is alone. A tragic, sad figure, she stands as a symbol of pure alienation.

Ingel-Lei, The Mountain Flower, also had a significant theme. A king falls in love with a beautiful maiden called Ingel-lei and wishes to make her his own; but there is a natural calamity with floods and much destruction and he has to turn to the needs of the people. The High Priest decrees that what the river wants is a human sacrifice and that the most desirable virgin in the land must be found for the purpose. Ingel-lei is the one selected and she is brought before the king. He is shattered and dazed. He tries to help her escape, but his plan fails. The ill-fated girl is led away to the sacrificial ritual watched by her helpless lover. Here, once again, is the Iphigenia myth so common to ancient peoples.

The beautiful Charu Mathur danced the heroine of the first ballet with great ability but it was as Ingel-lei that she was really moving, and the company's leader, Rajkumar Singhajit Singh, maintained his characteristically high standard of performance in the male lead of both ballets as well as in the other dances. Dani Singh's dancing as the Chief and the High Priest can only be described as powerful and meaningful.

One criticism: the person responsible for the map on the cover of the programme notes ought to brush up his geography. He seems to think that the area of Manipur is larger than that of the states of Assam and West Bengal put together. REGINALD MASSEY

Burma and India. The Dancing Times. LXI, 730, Jul 1971, p 530

16

Burma and India

by

REGINALD MASSEY

The photograph above of the Burmese National Dancers was taken by Frederika Davis. The drawing below is by one of the company.

AS PART OF THEIR FIRST VISIT TO WESTERN Europe, the Burmese National Dancers and Musicians appeared at the Wells from April 19th to May 1st. Their art is a happy synthesis of influences from India, Siam, Bali and Java and underlying all these is the natural gaiety and carefree spirit of the Burmese people who refuse to take too solemn a view of life but accept rather the world for what it is and make the best of it. No deep tragedies, conflicts, jealousies or bloody combats here; indeed, it could be argued that the lack of these elements in the repertoire resulted in too pretty a picture.

The sinuous arms, swaying hips, flexible wrists and coy smiles which were accompanied by the gong, oboe and drum conjured up a land of gold and precious gems where the flying fishes play. The dance ensemble of exotic girls in stockinged feet performing to the classical song *Sein Kyaung Nilar* was a good example of the lyrical nostalgia in which these superb artists specialise. *Anyein,* gentle grace, also pervaded the *Dance of the Oil Lamps* and the *Duets* whose theme was the pledging of undying love.

The lively male dances were full of leaps, spins and rolls and many had a strongly competitive bias. Of these I liked *Archery Contest, Deer Stalkers,* and the acrobatic *Dance on the Prop Chests;* but the best in this genre was *Rival Zawgyis.* The zawgyi is one who has succeeded in the attainment of all knowledge, especially that of the occult; he has discovered the philosopher's stone and can bring to life the beautiful tree maidens with one touch of his magical wand. In *Rival Zawgyis* two such beings meet. One is an aristocratic zawgyi and the other a country dweller and their efforts at one-up-

manship were a pleasure to behold. The dancers, U Tin Aung and U Than Sein, invested the dance with just the right amount of humour without making it banal.

Daw Khin Sein's solo *Obeisance Dance* was a masterpiece. Her body from the toes to the eyebrows slowly opened up, as it were, like a flower at sunrise, petal by petal, bowing in reverence to its maker and at the same time greeting its admirers. Here was dancing in one of its most exquisite forms.

Burmese marionette has a long and honoured tradition; puppets are manipulated to dance like humans and humans are "manipulated" to dance like puppets. It was altogether fascinating to watch the two puppeteers, U Shwe and U Tun Kyi, pulling, plucking and fingering the strings with inspired intensity.

The music for the dances was full of vitality and rich in sounds which were new and exciting although the piece played on the boat-shaped harp was disappointing in its naivety.

It is unfortunate that some of the choreography appeared to have been specially tailored for western audiences. I found this not only unnecessary but irksome.

Surya Kumari

INDIAN DANCE BY ITS VERY NATURE IS A composite art which involves training in mime, instrumental and vocal music, make-up, drama and yoga. London audiences got some idea of this composite quality when Surya Kumari appeared at the Purcell Room on June 16th and 19th. The Mahabharata, epic of war and religion, was presented in *nritya,* expression of sentiment and mood,

which led into the Vedic recitation of parts of the Gita, the Song Divine which the god Krishna is said to have delivered to mankind on a battlefield. After the Sanskrit, Surya Kumari recited in English. There were hymns ancient and modern from Shankaracharya to Tagore in Indian languages and English and many ragas, serious and light, which Surya Kumari will be issuing as an L.P. album later this year. The pure dance items were from the Bharata Natyam repertoire and also included the well known Cobra Dance, an exercise in movement and mime. Surya Kumari's new solo presentation, Vikramaditya, based on ancient legend, is a synthesis of dance, drama, music and the spoken word.

Gifted Canadian

BEFORE A SMALL AUDIENCE, ALAS, AT THE Commonwealth Institute Theatre on June 2nd Anjali presented items from the Bharata Natyam (southern Indian) and Odissi (eastern Indian) schools. Her clear line, verve and sense of *talam,* time measures, were quite outstanding especially in the *Tillana* which depicted poses from various temple sculptures: the arms, like flashes of lightning, would ignite a god into life and then, just as suddenly, freeze into another deity.

The unusual *padam,* danced poem, about a low caste devotee begging admittance into Shiva's shrine had tremendous possibilities but because Anjali could not summon up enough *nayanabhinaya,* expression through the eyes, much of the pathos escaped her. Anjali's forte, however, is the liquid flowing Odissi and chief among her dance in this style was a faintly erotic interpretation in which a *sakhi,* confidante, advises Radha on a meeting with the god Krishna.

Anjali ("Salutation with the hollowed palms of both hands") is the stage name of Anne-Marie Gaston, a Canadian, and the commendable standard of her dancing does credit to her and to her gurus, Mayadhar Raut for Odissi and Swarna Saraswati, Ellapa Pillai and Dakshinamurthy for Bharata Natyam.

India and Ceylon. <u>The Dancing Times</u>, LXI, 732, Sep 1971, p 654

India and Ceylon

by

REGINALD MASSEY

The photograph above by Pam Jones is of Kama Dev with his guru, Vempati Chinna Satyam, rehearsing at The Place.

THE VILLAGE OF KUCHIPUDI LIES IN INDIA'S Andhra State and has given its name to a dance-drama with a most interesting history. Sidhyendra Yogi, a saintly brahmin, can be called the founder of the dance-drama as we know it today. He was a devotee of Krishna and it is said that the lord appeared to him in a *darshan* or vision and asked him to write a play from the Krishna legends. Sidhyendra Yogi did as he was commanded but was left with the problem of staging the play. He could find neither sufficiently competent dancer-actors nor people willing to back him. Eventually, he arrived at Kuchelapuram, the village of his wife's family, on the banks of the river Krishna near the city of Masulipatnam. Here the brahmins, who were Krishna worshippers, agreed to help him. The dance-drama was a great success and after this they staged it every year as part of their religious festivals. The neighbouring villages also did likewise. In 1675, the Nawab of Golconda, Abdul Hassan Tahnisha, saw a performance by the Kuchelapuram brahmins and was so impressed that he granted the village and the surrounding lands to the dancers, with the stipulation that the tradition of the dance-dramas should be carried

on. This grant was inscribed on copper plate, which was the custom in south India symbolic of authority and perpetuity.

Through the years Kuchelapuram came to be called Kuchipudi—the name which attached itself to the dance—and in spite of many vicissitudes the dance tradition has survived to our own day. A descendant of one of the ten families who performed Sidhyendra Yogi's first dance-drama is the guru Vempati Chinna Satyam, who toured Europe recently with his pupil Kama Dev. They appeared at The Place on August 1st: Kama Dev dancing, Vempati Chinna Satyam conducting and singing and assisted by C. P Venkatesan (flute), S. R. Govindarajan (mridangam—the south Indian drum), and Kumar (drone instrument).

I said in the July issue of last year that Kama Dev was a dancer worth watching; now that he has spent another year with his great teacher I can say that he is among his country's leading young male dancers. Vempati Chinna Satyam has obviously done a lot for him: the first invocatory piece and *Ramapat-abhishekam*, recounting the god Ram's life, were danced with body and soul in a manner which would have warmed Lorca's heart. *Dasavataramul*, de-

picting the ten incarnations of Vishnu, was danced well enough but not as expressively as it was last year; the Krishna dance, with its difficult rhythmic steps on a brass salver, was a pleasure, as was the legend concerning a contest between an elephant and a crocodile. Kama Dev's real attainment, however, was seen in the final *Tillana*, pure dance item. Here *jatis*, rhythmic patterns, of 8 beats from the solo Bharata Natyam style alternated with 5 beat *jatis* of the Kuchipudi style. Not only did this demonstrate the difference between *jatis* of the two styles but it also emphasized their often subtle peculiarities.

Chitrasena

BUDDHISM, LIKE ANY OTHER PROSELYTIZING protestant religion, ran the risk of throwing out the baby with the bath water. Song, dance and music were looked upon with disfavour. A people's way of life, however, cannot really be radically altered and so the pre-Buddhist arts of the Kandyan hill kingdom of Ceylon flourished in spite of Buddhism being the state religion. Whereas the Kandyan dances maintained their purity— the kingdom survived till as late as 1815— the dances of the mid-lands and those of the maritime regions were debased to a large extent.

The Chitrasena Dance Company, founded twenty-five years ago by the dancer-choreographer Chitrasena, appeared at Sadler's Wells from August 10th-21st and presented items from the three Ceylonese styles. It became clear that in his enthusiastic resuscitation of these dances the choreographer had injected so many foreign elements that quite often their very character was changed. *Gajaga Vannama*, descriptive of an elephant, was highly Grahamesque while the ballet movements of *Ukussa (Hawk)* and *Devadatta and Hansa*, a *Swan Lake* story, were amateurish and naive. London has by now seen so much of the real thing that kitsch will just not do. Even the duet by Chitrasena and Vajira, where the Kandyan rhythms were adapted for the stage, did not come off: it was supposed to illustrate the *tandava*, masculine, and *lasya*, feminine, aspects of dance but only succeeded in a certain heaviness by the male partner and an unattractive leonine quality by the danseuse. What a pity! For Vajira has beauty, line and presence which were always apparent but had to dance against the odd choreography; like an exquisite hand in an ill fitting glove.

However, there were many good things as well; notable amongst which was the strong *Ves*, a propitiation dance, by seven male dancers in elaborate headdress. This was the real Kandyan style, virile and virtuoso. And then, of course, there were the drums. The sheer volume and hypnotic power of the drummers Suramba, Punchi Gura and Dineris would be difficult to equal.

Dervish Dancers. The Dancing Times. LXII, 736, Jan 1972, p 207

Dervish Dancers

AS PART OF THEIR WORLD OF ISLAM FESTIVAL the Oriental Centre presented the Mevlevi dervishes at Friends House, Euston, from November 18th - 25th. It was a happy idea to bring Islamic religious dance to London for the very first time, for the West has seen almost nothing of the dance of the Islamic countries. This particular group of thirty-five dancers and musicians came from Konya in Anatolia where their fraternity was founded by Jalal-uddin Rumi, one of the world's greatest mystic poets, in the thirteenth century. Rumi was called Mevlana (" Our Master ") and so the dervishes (the word derives from a Persian word signifying " poor ") who followed him came to be known as the Mevlevi. Rumi's brotherhood resembled the ascetic Christian orders in many ways but he placed great emphasis on the realisation of the Divine through the medium of music and dance.

Every item of the dervishes' costume is symbolic, as in their every movement, attitude or gesture. The long white robe represents the shroud, the black cloak the tomb, and the tall felt hat the tombstone. The red sheepskin rug on which the Sheikh, Selman Tuzun, sat evoked the sunset on the fateful day that Rumi died.

The dance ritual started with solemn unaccompanied singing by Kani Karaca in praise of the Prophet Mohammed. The atmosphere of reverence and mystery was further developed by the *ney* (flute) players led by the brilliant Niyazi Sayin. The Sheikh then struck the floor and the dervishes, advancing slowly, went round the dance area three times. These represented the three stages towards God: science and knowledge, understanding and vision, and the final union.

After divesting themselves of their black cloaks the dancers, with arms outstretched like wings, started whirling slowly. Almost imperceptibly the whirling increased in speed until a trance-like hypnotic state was achieved.

This last movement had a quality of ecstacy, a feeling of fulfilment. It was a religious experience in the truest sense.

REGINALD MASSEY

Korean Classics at The Place. <u>The Dancing Times</u>. LXII, 739, Apr 1972, p 373

Korean Classics
at
The Place

LONDON HAD A MARVELLOUS EXPERIENCE OF Korean culture when the distinguished dancer, actor, scholar and poet Won-Kyung Cho appeared at The Place from March 6th-11th. Dr. Cho prefaced his programmes with short, humorous explanations of the basic grammar of Korean as well as Chinese and Japanese art. What emerged was the revelation of a highly developed, complex and sophisticated system of æsthetics that had urged artists towards achievements not dissimilar to those of the great figures of the European Renaissance. Of the Buddhist inspired pieces Dr. Cho's own creation, *Secret Yearning,* was a minor masterpiece. It told of the frustrated love of a novice monk who decides to give up the ascetic life but who is plainly unprepared and unequipped for the rigours beyond the monastery walls. He is drawn back to the monastery and returns a repentant prodigal. A brilliant psychological study and one which summed up the failure of human desire.

The Confucian dance which is performed at the ancestral mausoleums of the highest dignitaries was, alas, all too brief. The slow regal movements, proud and solemn—accompanied by crashing, scraping music very reminiscent of electronic sounds—had a frightening, awe-inspiring effect not easily forgotten. Also outstanding were the two mask dances: one portraying a drunken old man trying to recapture his lost youth and the other a grotesquely funny puppet-like performance requiring incredible body control. Dr. Cho's interpretation of female roles was entirely convincing and mention must be made of *Chun Aeng Jon,* the nightingale dance, composed by King Ik Jong in the 18th century.

The *keesaengs,* cultivated courtesans and entertainers, were numbered amongst the intellectual elite of the country and Dr. Cho included a number of poems by them in his dramatic renderings of love poetry. Here was great lyrical verse by any standards: veined with pain, nostalgia and delicate imagery it spoke the language of sensibility. Dr. Cho is a considerable reciter and translator and he presented the poems in English, Korean, Chinese and Japanese. His selection of Korean poems in Japanese translation is due out soon. I wish he would do a similar service for the English speaking world.

REGINALD MASSEY.

Epics from India. The Dancing Times. LXII, 742, Jul 1972, pp 531-532

Epics from India

by

REGINALD MASSEY

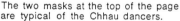

The two masks at the top of the page are typical of the Chhau dancers.

NON-VIOLENCE AS A CODE OF ETHICS WAS A relatively late arrival in the history of India. For it was only in the 5th century B.C. that Prince Siddharta, known later as the Buddha or the Enlightened One, founded a religion and a way of life based on non-violence, right action and charity. The *Ramayana* and the *Mahabharata,* the two pre-Buddhist epics, are much concerned with war, dynastic feuds and Good versus Evil, and provide a panoramic—if sometimes ambiguous—view of ancient India. These legends have been preserved in folk and classical dance forms, and London had examples of both when the Chhau dancers of Bengal appeared at Sadler's Wells from May 22nd-June 3rd and the Kathakali dance-drama company visited the Aldwych from May 15th-27th for this year's World Theatre Season. I have mentioned Chhau first advisedly, for in India the sophisticated arts have grown from and, indeed, have always been sustained by the traditional folk idioms.

It is a recent and welcome phenomenon that scholars and researchers in India have applied themselves to the vast wealth of folk art that still exists in that country. The Chhau masked dance of Purulia was thus discovered about a decade ago by the indefatigable Professor Bhattacharyya of Calcutta in a remote area of West Bengal. The dance-dramas are performed by the people themselves and not by professionals, as in the case of Kathakali, during the festivals of the Sun God. The participation of each group is of course clearly defined: the aborigines are the dancers, the low caste Hindus the drummers, and the higher caste Hindus make the masks for they are supposedly better qualified to portray the deities. The singer who tells the story of each play and who acts as a compère is also from a higher caste. Seeing these village folk, many of them illiterate, doing their own thing for the first time in a modern theatre would have been embarrassing had it not been for their devastating simplicity. There were loud voices off-stage; entrances and exits were muddled; the drummers issued instructions to each other after the curtain had gone up; the soloist of the oboe-like instrument seemed to have a grudge against the singer-compère for he insisted on starting his shrill notes before the singing had finished. And yet naïvely they carried on undisturbed and unhurried.

Two episodes, both about the untimely deaths of young men, stood out above the rest. The first told of how on the battlefield

On the left, one of the splendid mounted figures from the Chhau troupe.

of Kurukshetra (the Indian equivalent of the plains of Troy) the young Abhimanyu was slain by seven warriors of the opposing army; the second dealt with the sad circumstances leading to the accidental death of the god Krishna at the hands of a hunter. The scene with three women weeping over the body of the dead god was most moving.

Fertility rites the world over often demanded the sacrifice of a young person and I suspect that these two stories, coming as they do during the festivals of the Sun God, are connected with some forgotten fertility cult. The performers are agricultural people whose forebears must have performed ritual sacrifices to propitiate the Sun God, the giver of life, and it is possible that the original ceremony gradually gave way to this symbolic drama depicting the deaths of two most acceptable young men of high status.

Professor Bhattacharyya, Milena Salvini of the Association de Recherche d'Archéologie Théâtrale and Jean-Louis Barrault, to whose Théâtre des Nations they went after their sojourn here, did well to bring these dancers to the West. Nevertheless, I question whether they did equally well in presenting them in a conventional theatre. They should have been out in the open air stamping the good earth with their bare feet: a folk dance festival would have been their right milieu. The boards are not for them; their dance is too close to the soil.

"Theatre" is nowadays such an umbrella term that I suppose it was permissible to have Kathakali, Kerala's well-known dance-drama, on a theatre season bill. Kathakali is, nonetheless, both "dance" and "drama". And so when a conscious attempt is made to minimise the "dance", while at the same time highlighting the "drama", the result runs the risk of becoming lopsided. Add to this the task of editing and making "dramas" of suitable length out of night-long Kathakali performances and you get some idea of the problems involved. *Ramayana,* a very potted version of the real thing, had all the ingredients of a full-length play: Ravana the demon king of Lanka (Ceylon) abducts Sita, the wife of the exiled god-king Rama; Rama sets out to recover his wife and succeeds with the help of his monkey-god friend Hanuman; Ravana is killed and Rama brings Sita back to Bharata (India) where he takes his rightful throne and is crowned with much pomp. Ravana was danced (or shall I say played?) by Chathunny Panicker with relish and the great Krishnan Nayar performed his usual wonders as Bali, a monkey chief. The comic interlude between Bali and his brother Sugriva, danced very well by Kesavadev, was brilliant but the amount of time spent on it was out of all proportion to its significance in the plot. From the dramatic point of view this was a serious flaw since it held up the action no end. Thus from time to time the considerations that prevailed were either those of entertainment or those that

Two scenes from the Kathakali dramas that were presented at the Aldwych Theatre as part of the World Theatre season.

exploited a role for its own sake. Krishnan Nayar, for example, is justly famous for his portrayal of Ravana as a seducer. But did even Nayar's genius justify the producer in expending half an evening on what was virtually one seduction scene? And yet *Ravana's Outrage,* as it was titled, counted as a "play"; similarly *The Rake's Downfall* (I wonder who was responsible for that Hogarthian title) which showed the killing of the evil general Keechaka by the disguised

hero Bhima. Nayar, as Keechaka, had a magnificently lengthy death scene but the plot of the "play" was thin indeed.

As I indicated earlier, presenting Kathakali is no easy proposition, but that does not exonerate the inadequacies. However, there was at the Aldwych a wealth of talent, even some genius. The subject matter covered over the fortnight was rich and varied, and the dance-drama itself as an art form was, as ever, sophisticated and powerful.

22

Kabuki. <u>The Dancing Times</u>. LXII, 743, Aug 1972, p 584

The scene of Ninjo from Chushingura which the Kabuki Theatre performed at Sadler's Wells during their June season.

Kabuki

ORIGINATING IN THE LATTER PART OF THE 16th century, Kabuki—meaning " song and dance "—developed in Osaka and Tokyo and soon attained the status of popular dance theatre. The art form was first practised by women of easy virtue to advertise their charms; but when public performances by women were banned by law men took over. Thus started the profession of the female impersonator or *onna gata;* from early childhood selected boys were trained to specialise in female rôles and over the years this became an honoured calling.

Seen in London recently was Nakamura Utaemon VI—the greatest *onna gata* today and designated a living national treasure in Japan—who headed a company of 20 dancer-actors, 16 musicians and 14 technicians at the Wells where, from June 5-17, two pieces from the classical repertoire were presented. The first, *Chushingura (The Forty-seven Loyal Samurai)*, was based on historical fact and told of honour and revenge. We were shown only four of the eleven acts in which the chief characters are Moronao the evil governor of Kamakura, Lady Kaoyo whom he wishes to seduce, and Hangan, her husband. After being rebuffed by Lady Kaoyo, Moronao baits her husband and provokes him to violence. Now the use of violence in the palace is a capital offence and Hangan is sentenced to death; he must commit *seppuku,* that is, suicide by disembowelment. The *seppuku* ritual, serious and surgically precise, was performed without dramatic trimmings: it was the sheer truth of the action that made the impact. Later, Hangan's loyal samurai exact revenge for their master's death. Shikan VII played the wronged husband Hangan, Ganjiro II was Moronao and Utaemon VI was Lady Kaoyo. All did brilliantly.

However, what really moved was the second piece, *Sumidagawa (The Sumida River)*. In this Utaemon VI was the mother driven mad by the disappearance of her son. She searches for him everywhere and eventually, with the help of a boatman, finds the boy's grave by a river bank. She dances with joy, for her deranged mind conjures up a vision of the boy alive. But soon the vision passes and even she realises that it was a mere dream. The samisen music (music associated with Kabuki in which the samisen, a three-stringed instrument played with a plectrum, is all important) added to the vastness of the desolation and grief. It is no wonder that *Sumidagawa* was Britten's inspiration for *Curlew River.*

The sets were marvels of simplicity and imaginative design giving, as they did, clues for the eye and the mind to dwell upon.

The decision to stage only two items during a whole fortnight was an unfortunate one. Also some arrangement for simultaneous translation was essential: the sarcasm, recitation and clever dialogue in 17th century Japanese was wasted. Moreover, *Chushingura* was too long. Surely skilled editing could have pruned it down to half its length; the producers must know that by and large no audience can be expected to take so much of an idiom that is so alien. Few indeed are the dance mad, myself included, who would be prepared to wait ten minutes while Utaemon VI swayed ten steps and froze into an attitude of feminine pique.

REGINALD MASSEY

23

Beautiful Koreans. The Dancing Times. LXIII, 745, Oct 1972, p 21

Beautiful Koreans

by

REGINALD MASSEY

The photograph of the Koreans above was taken by Shuhei Iwamoto

WHAT A PLEASURE IT WAS TO SEE THE Koreans again when they descended on the Roundhouse from September 4 - 9 like a flock of vivacious, exotic birds. Many of them had appeared at The Place last year, but this time they came in a somewhat larger group, with a wider repertoire, under the banner of the Korean National Dance Company. They began with the elegant *Flower Crown Dance* and ended with the lively *Farmer's Dance*, which was full of rousing drums, pipes, gongs and swirling streamers. It was a good idea to divide the dances according to the seasons: and how appropriate that *Song of Love*, with its yearning and nostalgia, should have been allocated to Autumn. Kim, Moon-Sook danced the heroine with what I can only describe as a touch of genius and Song, Bum rose to the occasion as her partner. Earlier Madame Kim had performed another miracle in *Spring and Romance* with Chun, Hwang. Why this great danseuse was not given more to do I could not understand.

The singing from *pan-sori*, narrative opera, by Kim, So-Hee added a new dimension to the programme and the wonderful flautist Lee, Seang-Kang excelled himself on the *tai-keum*, the large Korean flute. The singing to the *kaya-keum*, the twelve-stringed zither, by Park, Kui Hee and her two companions was delightful. They first sang *Sae-taryung (Song of Birds)* and then *Jebi-nojunggi (Song of the Swallows returning from the South)*.

I wish the Koreans would return soon. I recommend them wholeheartedly—for the whole family, Grandmother included.

24

Persian Delights at the Wells. The Dancing Times. LXIII, 747, Dec 1972, pp 137-139

Persian Delights at the Wells

The Mahalli Dancers

by

REGINALD MASSEY

All the photographs of the Mahalli Dancers with this feature were taken by Anthony Crickmay in Iran.

PERSIA, OR TO GIVE THE EMPIRE ITS PROPER name—Iran—has always had a reputation for roses, poets, nightingales and beautiful people, and from November 6-18 the Iranians came to Sadler's Wells Theatre and proved that reputation well founded. The Mahalli Dancers, a company of fifty, under their founder-director Robert de Warren (ex-Royal Ballet, who has spent six years researching dance and music in Iran) chose London for their first ever appearance abroad: an honour which we appreciate. They presented what amounted to a mini-festival of dance, music and poetry in classical and folk idioms.

The range was wide in style as well as regional representation. From Baluchestan, the eastern province, there were dances by men and women which told simple folk tales rather in the manner of the folk dancers of Pakistan and those of Rajasthan in India. Also from Baluchestan came the dervishes of the Moulavi order, a brotherhood of Sufi mystics founded by the poet-saint Jalal-uddin Rumi in the thirteenth century. To the expressive chanting, by Ebrahimi, of Rumi's verses the dervishes whirled into a state of fine ecstasy. In contrast to this was the joyful clapping dance by women from Torbat-Jam which is situated near Afghanistan. Their men-folk responded with a virile sword dance. Then from Bojnurd, bordering on Soviet Russia, came graceful dances by both men and women.

The Turkomans, from north-eastern Iran, are ethnically related to the Mongols and their tribal dances were quite fascinating. The women while weaving their carpets moved to an insistent rhythm. The men emitted throaty and frightening growls—their only accompaniment apart from a lone singer—like the clap of distant thunder while performing their wide loping steps.

The best work dances were, however, from Guilan on the shores of the Caspian Sea. The Guilakis cultivate tea and rice and the movements of their daily tasks have been translated into dance. The Kurds, from the west, were another interesting group. Their dances celebrated a simple *joie de vivre* and the handkerchief dance was an absolute delight. In their mixed groups the men and women actually touched each other and such shedding of inhibitions is unusual in a society which frowns upon any physical contact between members of the opposite sex in public.

I was not impressed by the women's court

dances. They looked neither Iranian nor ballet: one of them, in fact, was distinctly night-clubbish. But the music was impressive throughout with wonderful contributions from the many drums, strings and woodwinds with special mention due to Mohammad Heidari's artistry on the *santur,* a zither-like instrument played by striking the wires with a pair of small sticks, and M.Ismaili's drumming on the wine glass shaped *zarb.* The poetry presentation was well done by Homa Partovi and Pavine Sarlak: the ladies recited impeccably in Persian while the English transliterations were delivered admirably by Cyrus Anvar in a rich timbre not unlike Sir John Gielgud's.

North Koreans. The Dancing Times. LXIII, 751, Apr 1973, p 374

26

NORTH KOREANS
by REGINALD MASSEY

THE MANSUDAI NATIONAL DANCE COMPANY OF the Democratic People's Republic of Korea were scheduled to appear at Sadler's Wells from March 12-24. However, since they were unable to get to London on time, they opened on March 15. The large troupe of 110 gave a varied programme of dance, music, and acrobatics that included lyrical, moving, humorous, and nationalistic pieces. Whatever they did was executed with precision—a prime example being the way in which three wood-wind instrumentalists marched on to the stage in identical dark suits with red lapel badges, played their exquisite music, and then, their work accomplished, marched off in single file. Quite obviously the training in Pyongyang instils discipline. Some, indeed, might argue that there was too much expertise and too little art. I would say that it's well nigh impossible to separate one from the other and, in any case, one has to understand that " art " does not mean the same thing to all men. There are, nevertheless, certain common areas of consent: the superb acrobatics, for instance. The split second timing, the line, the co-ordination, the daring, all added up to a kind of " art " that even we would recognize and readily applaud.

The celebratory dances such as *Apple Harvest, Bumper Harvest,* and *Spring* told of the fruits of labour and the joys of living. Pretty girls danced with the *changgo* (the hour-glass shaped Korean drum) and questioned the cuckoo about news of Spring. The colourful back projections of lush meadows, apples and apricots in bloom and playful waterfalls gave an impression of pastoral peace. But later there was a change of mood. *The Azaleas of the Fatherland* was an embarrassing piece of nationalism with a platoon of khaki-clad girls cavorting around with fistfuls of azaleas. The *Brief Introduction to Items of Performance* explained that this particular dance depicted " the boundless love of the pretty female soldiers for the fatherland " From this let it not be construed that I disapprove of nationalism, socialism, or even capitalism as subjects for dance. All are grist to the mill. What matters is the treatment and whether enough creative energy has been expended on the project to make it work. The *magnum opus* of this company is *Snow Falls* and this inspired creation has sweep, movement, deep feeling and elegance. It is a hymn to socialist aspirations and the realization of the promised city. In spite of the snow and the blizzards the workers forge forward to achieve, finally, clear skies with the Sun illuming the firmament. Neither the indifferent programme notes nor the above-mentioned *Brief Introduction* gave credit to the choreographer of this dance. Let us congratulate him or her.

To end, I wish to say that I was bitterly disappointed by a grave lacuna in the dance programme, varied though it was. There was not a single religious dance to be seen. Buddhism has given Korea many dances but the Mansudai Company consigned to oblivion that significant part of Korea's heritage. Is it wise for any national dance company to forget dance history?

27

Bayanihan. <u>The Dancing Times</u>. LXIII, 754, Jul 1973, p 542

Bayanihan

by

REGINALD MASSEY

BAYANIHAN STANDS FOR THE SPIRIT OF WORK-ing together and is a very suitable name for the Philippine National Dance Company which came to the Wells from May 29 to June 9. The dancers and musicians quite obviously enjoyed themselves hugely and their infectious *joie de vivre* permeated every part of the hall. Even so, this could not disguise the fact that significant sections of the programme were pretty small beer. The worst in this respect was that titled *Ecos de la Ermita* which was supposed to show scenes from the aristocratic quarter of old Manila. What we were served up were poor Spanish numbers with dollops of Miss Julie Andrews. The *Jota Manilena* was an adaptation of the *Castilian Jota* with castanets made of bamboo and not strung together. *Promenada*, I suppose, did have its moments.

The tribal pieces from the Mountain Province were pleasing. The Kalinga warriors, the girls pounding rice and fetching water in earthen pots, the wedding dance and the initiation ceremony—all had an air of authenticity. Lucrecia Reyes Urtula, the choreographer, has pioneered the presentation of these little known dances and I must congratulate her on her achievements. Later, the Arabic and Indo-Malayan influences on the Philippines were evident in the section called *Mindanao Tapestry. Magigal* and *Paunjalay* for example, both nuptial dances, were very Indian in concept and movement. Two famous dances of the " clacking bamboo " genre, *Singkil* and *Tinikling,* were

rapturously received. The performers danced in and out of many pairs of rapidly clapped bamboo poles. In *Singkil* we saw a prince courting a princess who was followed by an attendant carrying an umbrella and in *Tinikling* the dancers represented long-legged birds which frequent flooded paddyfields and which farmers attempt to trap. Another skilful dance was the all male *Maglalatik* for which hard coconut shells are tied to various parts of the body and legs, the virile dancers beating out rhythms on the shells as they leap and turn. Then there was the beautiful *Tinolabong*, the dance of the herons.

The programme notes were somewhat curious. On the title page no less than 13 credits were given, from the President of the Company to the combined office of Company Physician and Personnel Director, yet there wasn't a single dancer amongst that august lot. Towards the end there were biographies of six of the 13 V.I.P's; and at the very end, in small print, were the names of the dancers—splendid names such as Maria Theresa Mateo, Purification Yuhico and Fernando Jose Sison III. We were told nothing about them, nor were we told anywhere who danced what part. This was irritating. Who, I'd like to know, was that gorgeously attractive creature who danced the attendant in *Singkil* and who excelled again and again in dance after dance?

28

Mohini Attam. <u>The Dancing Times</u>. LXIV, 762, Mar 1974, p 338

Mohini Attam

in the

Purcell Room

by

REGINALD MASSEY

her competence in *abhinaya*, expression. Moving on to the male Kathakali style, Tara Rajkumar eloquently demonstrated the nine basic sentiments of Indian dance. However, acting the part of the demoness Putana was clearly far beyond her range. She would do well to avoid the dark, dramatic roles.

The other dancers in the programme were Savitri Nair and Kumari Valli. The latter performed only a short invocatory piece and one wonders why she was included at all. Miss Nair, on the other hand, did six items all of which were danced to taped music. Her Kuchipudi pieces were fairly passable and the Shiva dance in the Bharata Natyam style had its rare moments. Her *Thillana* in the Bharata Natyam idiom, which was meant to be scintillating, was miserable.

I have said before—and must perforce repeat—that organizers of Indian recitals ought to be a little more professional in their productions. This particular production was abysmal: the lighting was downright bad, the microphone levels were not adjusted, the tape recorder gave trouble, the announcements—when audible—were unintelligible, and the programme notes eventually arrived during the interval. Under such conditions it is a miracle that dancers retain their sanity let alone their ability to dance.

MOHINI ATTAM IS NAMED AFTER THE seductress supreme of Hindu mythology who enticed away the demons and thus helped the gods to gain possession of *amrita,* the elixir of life. Mohini had the graceful curves of the vine, her limbs shone with the full golden bloom of youth and her face enchanted all who looked upon it. Mohini Attam, therefore, is a very feminine dance style and it is not surprising that it became the preserve of the courtesans. The dance flourished in the south-western Indian states of Travancore and Cochin for a long time but, with the emergence of a puritanical and vocal middle class in India, there was an outcry against Mohini Attam and the princes were forced to ban it. Later, when the dance was almost extinct, the poets Vallathol and Tagore managed to exert their influence to reinstate it. In Cochin the ban was finally lifted in 1950. Among the few surviving exponents of Mohini Attam was Kalyani Amma, who passed on the tradition to a number of dancers. Shanta Rao, Mrinalini Sarabhai, Roshan Vajifdar and Kanak Rele have since revived Mohini Attam.

The beautiful Tara Rajkumar, one of Kalyani Amma's pupils, appeared in the Purcell Room on February 1 and conveyed some of the magic and allurement of this dance style. She used her eyes marvellously in the dance dedicated to the god Padmanabha in which the spurned woman, like the *chataka* bird longing for rain, languishes in unrequited love. Her *Dashavataram*, describing the ten incarnations of Vishnu, displayed once again

29

Dancers from Pakistan. <u>The Dancing Times</u>. LXV, 778, Jul 1975, p 535

Dancers from Pakistan

by

REGINALD MASSEY

The photograph at the top of the page is a group of girls dancing the *Jhoomer* from Sind. Below, the Khattak comes from the Khyber area of the North West Frontier. Traditionally performed by tribesmen, the dance is allied to the *rumal*, handkerchief, dances of Iran.

THE NATIONAL DANCE ENSEMBLE of Pakistan, directed by the gifted Zia Mohyeddin, appeared at the Commonwealth Institute Theatre on May 20. From the outset let me record that never have I seen a better produced programme from the India-Pakistan subcontinent. There was professional expertise at every level of production, an example to others of how "ethnic" dance from distant parts ought to be presented.

The eleven musicians were on stage throughout the evening and were most imaginatively used. The dancers — excellently deployed — flitted, pirouetted, stamped, clapped and sang with a joy that was truly infectious. The items, from the various regions of Pakistan, were either choreographed interpretations of the original forms or creative translations of them. However, Mohyeddin and his choreographers, Raffi Anwar, Nazir Ahmed and Bennet Naeem, marvellously retained the rustic spirit and, indeed, this is no mean achievement when one sees the folk dance of many countries being so vilely used for the greater glory of tourism.

The *Khattak* from the Khyber area and the *Bhangra* from the Punjab were lively pieces, the latter having a long pair of tongs, the *chimta*, to help with the rhythm. Baluchistan was represented by the *Leva*, very African in its movements and drumming, and the fishermen's dance from the Makran coast. The stick dance had obvious affinities with the *Garba* of Gujerat in India although the music was too Western and less than pleasing. The *Jhoomer*, from Sind, told of the exploits of Jamal Khan Rind, a legendary warrior, and was in many ways the most attractive of the folk dances. Of the creative pieces, *Moenjodaro*, was the best and *Nocturne*, with its use of south Indian *Bharata Natyam* movements, the least successful.

The sole classical dance was a fantastic *Kathak* item by Nahid Siddiqui, an artist of considerable talent. She has both charm and strength and I have no doubt that if she got the opportunity of studying *abhinaya*, expression, from a teacher such as Birju Maharaj of the Lucknow *gharana*, school, she could very easily become one of the subcontinent's leading dancers. Birju Maharaj, however, is in India and there's the rub. Instances such as this confirm my belief that some sort of cultural exchange between India and Pakistan is urgently called for. Artistic agreement between the two countries can achieve nothing but good.

Dances from India. The Dancing Times. LXVI, 781, Oct 1975, p 27

30

Dances from India

by

REGINALD MASSEY

THE FOUR JHAVERI sisters, Nayana, Ranjana, Suverna and Darshana, have over the years worked extremely hard for the cause of Manipuri dance which originated in north-east India. Their teacher, Guru Bipin Singh, has been a guiding influence but the credit for streamlining the staging and presentation must go to the Jhaveris, especially Nayana. Darshana, the youngest sister, has now become a most accomplished dancer and what a pleasure it was to see her on June 30 and July 1 and 3 at the Q.E.H. and on July 8, 9 and 10 at the Round House. She was the chief attraction of the Festival of Arts of India and her accompanying Manipuri dancers were Bir Mangal Singh and Shantibala Devi. Their repertoire was far ranging; from the powerfully masculine to the delicately feminine, from the deeply spiritual to the extrovertly joyful. It would be difficult to see anywhere, apart from Manipur itself, such a variety of Manipuri dance.

The *pung*, drum, was always used to good effect by the two female dancers but it was only when they were joined by Bir Mangal Singh — also with a *pung* — that the audience was enthralled by the incredible grace and vigorous virtuosity of the drum dances. In *Abhisarika* the delectable Darshana was Radha, fearful of many dangers, slipping through the forest for a tryst with her lover Krishna. Here was acting and dancing woven into a fine tapestry. With Shantibala Devi she performed *Lai Haroba*, the sacred dance ritual of the *maibis* or priestesses of Manipur and, in a less serious vein, she did wonders as the playful Krishna.

South India was represented by V.P. and Shanta Dhananjayan. Their style of Bharata Natyam is typical of the Kalakshetre school: classical and correct. It could, however, do with some warm moisture of humanity. The miming was almost mechanical and that is why their expressive dances did not really communicate very much in terms of inner feeling. Nevertheless, the Dhananjayans excel in pure dance and would have been well advised to have included more rhythmic pieces in their programme. Their *Thillana* duet, brilliantly choreographed, ranks among the best of its genre.

V.P. Dhananjayan's Kathakali dances were a peculiar mixture of the Bharata Natyam and Kathakali styles. He performed them without the slightest attempt at dancing on the outer edges of the feet which is characteristic of Kathakali, and this marred his stance and basic posture. The absence of the appropriate costume and make up which should have revealed the complexities of this style, here served only to reduce further the resemblance to Kathakali.

On the whole the South Bank evenings were aesthetically less satisfying than those at Chalk Farm even though the presentation and introductions at the Round House could have been more professional. At both places one looked in vain for the Kathak dancer so prominently displayed on the Festival's pamphlets and posters.

I have in the past written about foreigners who have attained high competence in Indian dance. One such is Anne-Marie Gaston, a Canadian whose professional name is Anjali. On July 29, she danced Odissi, Bharata Natyam and Kuchipudi at the Ewen Hall, Barnet. Her programme, a highlight of the forward looking Barnet Festival, brought out very clearly the main differences between the three styles. Anjali's Kuchipudi is delightful and her *Manduka Shabdam,* which told of the beautiful maiden Mandodari who was turned into a frog, deserves special mention.

Darshana, the youngest of the well-known Jhaveri sisters, in Manipuri male costume.

31

Uday Shankar. <u>The Times</u>. 29 Sep 1977

UDAY SHANKAR

Mr Reginald Massey writes:

Uday Shankar, the most original and celebrated dancer-choreographer of modern India, died in Calcutta on September 26 at the age of 77.

In the history of dance he will be remembered for the professional standards he set for Indian ballet, and for evolving a new style influenced by both East and West yet clearly Indian and unmistakably stamped with his own peculiar genius.

The eldest son of a distinguished Bengali Brahmin family from Jessore, now in Bangladesh, he came to England at the age of 18 to study at the Royal College of Art under Sir William Rothenstein. The young Shankar was noticed by Pavlova at a charity dance recital in London. His striking stage presence and his face, figure, and movements epitomized for her the dance of the East. She was fascinated. He helped her to choreograph *The Hindu Wedding* and *Radha and Krishna* and danced Krishna to her Radha.

After 18 months he launched out on his own in Paris and while there made a careful study of the art and culture of many countries. Later he based his company at Dartington Hall from where he toured the world, introducing Indian dance to distant parts.

In 1938 Shankar returned home and founded his India Culture Centre at Almora in the Himalayan foothills. He staffed it with the foremost teachers of various styles of Indian dance and music, the most notable among them being Allauddin Khan, the mentor of Shankar's younger brother Ravi.

At Almora, Shankar nurtured a galaxy of talent, which, in later years, profoundly influenced the performing arts of his country. His own balletic creations such as *Labour and Machinery, The Rhythm of Life* and *Samanya Kshati* injected new subject matter into Indian dance. More recently, however, he was criticized by the orthodox purists for having the audacity to innovate and fashion was in their favour. He died largely disillusioned but a lord of dance nonetheless.

32

The Wells of Eastern Promise. <u>The Dancing Times</u>. LXVIII, 805, Oct 1977, p 30

The Wells of Eastern Promise

by

REGINALD MASSEY

The picture on the right illustrates the topengs which are the mask dances of Bali. Here Anak Agung Gede Oka, the dance prince, performs *Topeng Jauk* in which he "becomes" the legendary demon Jauk. The topengs are connected with ancestor worship and are pre-Hindu in origin.

SADLER'S WELLS justified its position as the prime shopwindow for foreign companies when *Les Danses Sacrèes de Bali* (August 1-13), *Kabuki* (August 15-27) and the Korean National Dance Company (August 30-September 10) appeared there with varying degrees of success.

The Balinese, from the village of Sebatu and discovered by Jacques Brunet, were led by the veteran dancer Anak Agung Gedé Oka, a prince for whom dancing is a part of family tradition. His *topengs,* mask dances, were superb. In *Topeng Dalem-Topeng Tua,* he used two masks, one to portray youth and the other to show age, and in *Topeng Jauk* he became as it were the fearsome demon Jauk. The other dancer of note was Wayan Pasek Yusabawa who, in *Baris Kreasi,* showed admirable virtuosity with his eyes and facial expressions. The influence of India was much in evidence, which is not surprising since Bali was Hinduized as early as the first century.

The girl dancers were uninspiring as was the musical content and the general standard of presentation was quite disappointing.

In comparison the *Kabuki* company led by Ichikawa Ennosuke III were faultless. They excelled in every department of dance drama and theatre art. *The Mansion of Kawazura*

Hogen told of how a fox took the form of a faithful warrior and how, in the end, he was restored to his own body. It was a tale full of sound and fury, signifying many things. Ennosuke III danced Tadanobu the fox and it was a moving experience to witness the tragic drama of a benighted animal acted out in human terms. In *Kurozuka* Ennosuke III danced the man-eating demon of Adachiga-hara, nearly converted to the non-violence of the Buddha. The proselytizing priest was Ichikawa Monnosuke VII while his low-born servant Tarogo was Ichikawa Danshiro IV. This strange dance drama was pervaded with a powerful sense of rectitude which, at crucial moments, was starkly silhouetted like a mountain peak outlined by lightning. In the end the demon was defeated but not converted and the villain, in fact, proved to be the nosy and all too human Tarogo who could not keep his bond with the demon.

The *samisen* music was marvellous throughout as were the *taiko,* drum, and *tsuzumi,* hand drum.

The Koreans presented, as they did five years ago, a good family show. (My son Marcus, aged 6½, enjoyed every minute of it.) Not for them the dark nights of the soul; they celebrated rather the song of birds awakening the land of the morning calm. Their choreography was uncomplicated and their girls beautiful one and all. Verily one would need the wisdom of a Solomon to single out any one of them. The group efforts, *Flower Crown Dance, Flower Fan Dance, Mask Dance,* and *Exorcist Dance,* were quite delightful. Among the solo items I liked best the *Pansori* operatic extract by Kim Dong-Ae and the *Sal-pu-li* dance of dream-like ecstasy by the enchanting Hong Keum-San to the accompaniment of the *kayakeum,* a twelve-stringed zither-like instrument.

I must insert a cautionary note here. The Koreans will in some quarters be accused of lacking content, being pretty pretty, too sweet, and even touristic. But if it is within the province of dance to be, at times, simply beautiful, graceful, and a pleasure to behold, then they are among the best.

On the left, Ichikawa Ennosuke III as the fox Tadanobu in the Kabuki dance drama *The Mansion of Kawazura Hogen.* Right, the Korean girls in one of their charming fan dances.

33

Kuchipudi Classics. The Dancing Times. LXVIII, 807, Dec 1977, p 157

Kuchipudi Classics

by

REGINALD MASSEY

The photograph above is of Raja and Radha Reddy in a Kuchipudi dance drama; it demonstrates the balance of strength and beauty in this style.

THAT WONDERFUL pair Raja and Radha Reddy did a whirlwind tour of Britain during October, taking almost literally in their stride places as far apart as Dartington Hall and the Nottingham Playhouse.

Their dance style is *Kuchipudi* which takes its name from a village in Andhra Pradesh, the Telugu speaking state in South India. The Reddys come from Andhra and both have had a long and arduous period of training under Guru Prahlada Sharma and Guru Krishna Sharma. The Reddys are today the leading performers of *Kuchipudi*. My wife, Jamila, introduced and explained some of their programmes to appreciative audiences in and around London. These were at Lambeth Town Hall (October 6), the I.C.A. (October 9), Christ's Hospital Arts Centre, Horsham (October 11), the Commonwealth Institute Theatre (October 14), and Jackson's Lane Community Centre (October 15).

Each performance was varied, well thought out and carefully presented, and due importance was given to lighting and acoustics — a refreshing change from what one usually gets in Indian dance programmes. Moreover, the Reddys are in peak form: in item after item they demonstrated virtuosity, expression, and a talent for choreographically editing the dance dramas to manageable length. An outstanding example of this was *Usha Parinayam*

which in its original setting often spans three nights. It is the story of Usha, a princess, who sees a lotus-eyed prince in a dream and falls in love with him. Her companion Chitrarekha teases her but eventually, through the power of her magic, transports the prince Anirudha to Usha's bedchamber. Usha recognizes her dream lover and they are united in eternal bliss. Raja Reddy was the prince and Radha Reddy danced both Usha and Chitrarekha. *Usha Parinayam,* in the Reddys' version, had charm, feeling and touches of humour.

Of the solo pieces Radha's *Intinoyamma* and *Krishna Shabdam* were perfectly coquettish and Raja's *Shiva Dance* and *Tripura Samhara Shabdam* adequately menacing. I say adequately since *Kuchipudi* does not lend itself easily to the powerful dramatic roles in the same way as, for instance, *Kathakali*.

The musicians, V. Sadasivam (*nattuvanar,* conductor), Lalita Nagarajan (vocalist), T. G. S. Gopalan (flautist), and N. N. Rao (*mridangist,* percussionist7, were first class throughout. Derry Barbour was responsible for sound and lighting. Incidentally, I've made a discovery in the Christ's Hospital Arts Centre at Horsham (director, Alan Wilkinson). Set in salubrious surroundings near the school, its new theatre is marvellous. A place with distinct possibilities.

Indian and Balinese Dancing in London

by

REGINALD MASSEY

THE KATHAKALI dancers from Kerala in south India appeared at Sadler's Wells Theatre from May 15-27 under the celebrated Krishnan Nair who is the only Kathakali artist to be honoured by the Indian government with the title of *Padma Shri*. The dance dramas are of inordinate length, lasting as they do for the best part of eight nights. Editing these works is no mean task for that is what must be done if Kathakali is to be staged in a normal theatre during generally acceptable theatre-going hours. It is on this score that many Kathakali presentations fail. However, Krishnan Nair surmounted this initial hurdle superbly. The three programmes, *Ramayana, Mahabharata,* and *Sons of Pandu,* were not only abbreviated but also made intelligible to those unfamiliar with the meanderings, intrigues and intricacies of Hindu myth and legend. Nair's early tours with Madame Stan Harding have obviously made him conscious of the fact that India's labyrinthine ways have to be made less labyrinthine.

Now sixty-five, Nair still has vitality and expression and he proved this by his tremendous portrayals of three quite distinctive characters. In *Ramayana* he was Ravana the demon king of Sri Lanka who had carried off Sita, the wife of the man-god Rama. In *Mahabharata,* the best edited of the three, Nair danced Kichaka the wicked general and in *Sons of Pandu* he was the mighty Bhima, second of the five heroic Pandava brothers, well meaning but not over intelligent. To each of these rôles Nair brought the wealth of his vast experience.

I spoke to him at the London home of Tara Rajkumar, one of his pupils who now lives here. Nair stressed the point about the variety of parts that Kathakali has to offer and the use of its dramatic potential in other forms of dance and drama. He has, in fact, recently worked with Peter Brook in Paris.

It was, however, in the area of theatricality that the Sadler's Wells season was disappointing and the blame must lie with Milena Salvini, the artistic adviser. No effort was made to set up the stage. The lighting, so vital in Kathakali as it is about good and evil, was miserable. Someone placed the traditional oil lamp upstage: it wasn't lit, and nobody bothered to explain the presence of the object. One of the cast who held up the colourful *therissila,* curtain, was clearly so fond of his

20th century watch that he could not be parted from it even while participating in something from the 17th century and no attempt was made to conceal the fact that all the thrones and seats had been borrowed from the theatre bar. Since this is not meant to be a piece of comic writing the catalogue of offences will not be continued.

Kathakali has always been the preserve of the Nair caste. But even in India things are changing. This company included a Brahmin, N. V. Nambudiri, who danced Bali and Vashista in *Ramayana* and a Muslim, Hyderali. As one of the two vocalists Hyderali sang and recited from the Hindu texts which he did admirably well. This is as if an orthodox Jew were serving at a Roman Catholic mass. Don't be shocked. That's India.

*   *   *

ALSO at Sadler's Wells there appeared, from June 5-17, a most interesting group of dancers and musicians from the village of Sawan in north Bali. They were brought over to Europe at considerable personal expense by Pierre Blanchard, a Frenchman with an ear for music and an eye for dance. The presentation was, to say the least, of a high standard. Bali's dance takes much of its inspiration from ancient India, but today's India can certainly learn a thing or two from Bali. The programmes were divided into four parts: palace and temple dances, excerpts from heroic ballets and instrumental pieces.

Topeng Tua, a classical mask dance by Gede Manik, depicted the problems of old age. An old man, toiling along under the merciless sun, is tormented by lice. He has no shelter and he cannot rid himself of the parasites that make his life unbearable. A

piece well observed and, in many ways, poignant.

Arjuna Wiwalia, "the marriage of Arjuna", told of the hero who, overcoming seduction by the nymphs, eventually slew the evil one and married the ideal woman. Arjuna was danced by the remarkable Konang Anggreni who also displayed great strength in the final *Baris* dance in which a warrior prepared himself, mentally and physically, for battle. Miss Anggreni has beauty and versatility and, with proper guidance and promotion, should go far.

The *guru* of the group was Gede Risi and the other dancers who did well were Ketut Suni, Komang Neli, Loh Priani, Dayu Kartika, Gusti Anom, Cening Murdita, Ketut Darmadi, Made Nurayati, Made Svamba, Ketut Tantra and Putuh Svarni.

The Q.E.H. was the venue of an Indian music and dance festival on June 12, 16, 17 and 18. The four dancers were Tirath Ajmani and Shovana Narayan (Kathak), Kumari Leela (Bharata Natyam) and Madhavi Mudgal (Odissi). From the outset let me say what a pleasure it was to see how admirably these young artists worked together. Although they have been trained under famous *gurus,* none of them comes from a traditional family of dancers and this may possibly have something to do with their openness and co-operative instincts. There were two memorable music and dance ensembles: in one, the moods of the four seasons were vividly expressed, and in the other the morning, the noon and the evening of a particular day were portrayed. Each performer danced to the appropriate *raga* in his or her own style and on occasion they danced in unison.

Individually, Tirath Ajmani and Shovana Narayan could not be faulted. His sequence describing the duel of Rama and Ravana was vigorously danced and her piece about the disrobing of Draupadi was unusual and evocative. Together, their Mughal court dance set the stage afire.

As usual with these Indian festivals, the production was almost amateurish and the speeches too long. However, the dancers were always ably supported by the following musicians: Meera Khirwadker (vocalist), Partho Das (sitar), P. Vasant Kumar (veena), Allauddin Khan (esraj and tar shehnai), Manika Prasad, the well-known table player, S. Rajeshwari (vocalist), T. R. Moorthy (flute), Trinath Maharana (pakhawaj), Hari Shankar Rai (vocalist), Shafat Ahmed (tabla), Madhup Mudgal (vocalist), and P. T. Ambalam (mridangam). This last young musician, I must sadly record, died suddenly while on tour, and although the troupe was in mourning this in no way affected their performances.

Eastern Delights

by

REGINALD MASSEY

Right, Guru Ammanur Madhava Chakyar demonstrates techniques of expression in the Kutiyattam style of dance drama.

THE Festival of India continued unabated during June and July and for the very first time London saw Kutiyattam, a form of dance drama from Kerala in south-west India. The guru brought over was the versatile Ammanur Madhava Chakyar, who was accompanied by Ammanur Parameshwaran, his nephew and leading pupil. At the Purcell Room on June 24 there was a demonstration of teaching techniques, and fascinating viewing this proved to be. Kutiyattam dates from the 8th century, and preserves elements of ancient Sanskrit theatre as opposed to the later and more popular Kathakali, which uses the regional language, namely Malayalam. Also, Kutiyattam depends to a far greater extent on the processes of recitation. Both styles were presented at the Riverside Studios on July 26 and 27, when lengthy excerpts from traditional dramas were enacted. In *Bali Vadham* the two brothers Bali and Sugriva are involved in a bloody dispute as to who should rule the country. Bali wins the first round and Sugriva retreats into the mountains. There Sugriva befriends the man-god Rama who, in due course, slays Bali. An interesting little tale but Ammanur Madhava Chakyar, in the role of Bali, invested it with dignity and tragedy. The final death scene, however, was intolerably long and should this Kutiyattam group ever come to these shores again I would strongly advise them to cut out three-quarters of it. Indeed, I am surprised that the Indian Council of Cultural Relations in New Delhi did not advise them likewise. Death scenes that go on *ad nauseam* can seriously rupture cultural relations when half the audience starts to doze off and the remaining half are too polite either to boo or giggle.

The Kathakali company, under their guru Ramankutty Nair were in tandem, as it were, with their seniors, the Kutiyattam artists. Their programmes were well edited and one enjoyed the amorous dalliance of Bhima and Draupadi and, after that, the humbling of the hero Bhima by the monkey-god Hanuman. Shri Venu, the dance scholar from Kerala, was an asset to both groups and it was a wise bureaucrat who decided to send him.

The Academy of Indian Dance — based at the Commonwealth Institute — organised a dance seminar on the last two days of June, followed by three successive performance nights. On July 1 Chitra Sundaram's artistic merit was discernible in spite of very many production errors. I saw her in Bombay some years ago when she was a student and mentioned her potential in the *Dancing Times* of November 1974. Her *Varnam,* composed by Chokkalingam Pillai, showed Chitra's grasp of the expressionistic aspects of Bharata Natyam and her *Thillana* was a cascade of pure rhythm which made the best use of her perfect proportions of neck, arms and legs. Tara Rajkumar's Kathakali programme the next night came up to a very high standard. In *Poothana-Moksham* she danced the demoness Poothana with commendable strength and

what I particularly liked in this interpretation was the emphasis given to the conflict in Poothana's mind as to whether she should poison the infant Krishna. She eventually decides to do her duty and to commit murder. The babe, however, being a god, suckles the very life out of her but pardons and grants her salvation just before she dies. In *Bhasmasura-Mohini* Bhasmasura the tyrant gets so big-headed that he even takes on the gods but Vishnu, assuming the form of the divine enchantress Mohini, lures him to destruction. Bhasmasura (K. Chandrasekharan) and Mohini (Tara Rajkumar) were excellently delineated but had the lighting been more skilfully used we would have got magic which was sadly missing from this otherwise well-danced piece. The third night was devoted to Kathak and Odissi by the Pawars but due to another commitment I could not attend as, with similar chagrin, I was unable to see Chitra Sundaram again at the Bharatiya Vidya Bhavan on July 24.

The Sanskritik Festival on the South Bank (July 5-July 10) and at various centres in the regions had a generally good quality this year even though there were irritating programme clashes. Guru Babu Singh Thingbaijam led the Manipuri dancers and drummers, and what a joy it was to see these charming hill folk! A similar pleasure was available at the Barbican Arts Centre from July 6-August 22. Here — as part of the Aditi multi-media event under the direction of Rajeev Sethi — were wedding dancers from Rajasthan and on seeing them one felt the very heartbeat of India. But back to Birendra Shankar's South Bank pre-

sentations. A pleasant surprise was Malavika Sarukkai, a young Odissi dancer who will have to be careful that her head isn't turned by silly accolades such as "India's leading dancer of Odissi". I do, however, feel fairly confident that given a few years of hard work she might well become just that.

Yamini Krishnamurti, the Bharata Natyam and Kuchpudi dancer, had a full night's programme on July 8 at the QEH and on July 30 she was presented by Nadabrahman in the Great Hall of Imperial College. On the evidence of both nights — but particularly of the second — I have no hesitation in stating that she is still India's leading Bharata Natyam dancer. The strong Kalakshetra line, the immense stamina and the charisma are all there to behold and to marvel at. Her *Varnam* to Lord Someswara was a masterpiece. At one moment there was tenderness, at another pride, at yet another lasciviousness. Her arms flashed like the sword of a Samurai and her eyes wrought destruction. Here was direct communication. Barriers of culture and language were trampled into the dust by the sheer strength of her artistry. This is not "pointless" dancing as the critic of *The Times* would have us believe. It is rather dancing that is at once earth-bound, abstract, significant to the human condition but well suited to imaginative flight. And it is precisely on account of these qualities that Pavlova and many other dancers after her went to India for inspiration.

It is true that at the QEH Yamini Krishnamurti was poorly served by the production, the confusing programme notes and the sickening sycophancy of the compère. Also, Kuchipudi certainly has sections — such as the interlocking of the great toes and the acrobatics on a salver — which descend to the level of bazaar entertainment and an artist of Yamini Krishnamurti's stature and creativity could and should dispense with such aesthetic offences.

Left, Chitra Sundaram executes a fast rhythmic movement in the *Thillana*, an exciting dance in the south Indian classical Bharata Natyam style.

36

Tribute to Bharati. The Dancing Times. LXXIII, 869, Feb 1983, p 383

Tribute to Bharati

BHARATI the Tamil poet was born in 1882 and is highly regarded as a visionary whose catholic and humanitarian interests were well in advance of his times. This emerged very clearly during the Bharati centenary celebrations held in London last December thanks to the efforts of Nadabrahman, the Indian High Commission and various other bodies in India. There was a literary symposium and a concert by the well known vocalist K. J. Yesudas. Padma Subrahmanyam, the distinguished south Indian dancer, came over specially to participate in the celebrations and she staged an exquisite tribute to the poet at the Logan Hall on December 11. Though the choreography was Dr. Subrahmanyam's (she has a doctorate in dance) the dance material was Bharati's. She had, in effect, strung together "poetic pearls of the quintessential Bharati".

Her Varnam, based on the poet's *Kuyil Pattu* (Song of the Cuckoo) was a gem using as it did both the *tandav* (strong and masculine) and the *lasya* (soft and feminine) aspects of the dance which she prefers to call Bharata Nrityam rather than Bharata Natyam. The cuckoo narrated the story of her previous births and in the one that Padma Subrahmanyam set to dance the bird was a hunter's daughter with whom a prince had fallen in love. The girl refused to be a mere mistress or concubine and the prince had to marry her with due respect in the presence of elders.

Bharati, a passionate believer in the dignity of womanhood, was an early campaigner for women's rights — long before the advent of Ms. Germaine Greer and her friends.

He was, above all, a devotee of Shakti which could be taken to mean divine power or eternal Mother. This conception was marvellously portrayed by Padma Subrahmanyam when she danced *Oozhikoothu (Dance of Destruction)* with a strange mesmeric power. The Thillana, again inspired by a Bharati poem, reflected the writer's unbounded optimism and his ability to see beauty in all of God's creations.

The singers were Shyamala Balakrishnam and Vijaya Natarajan. The mridangam was played by Padmaraj, the violin by Babu and the veena by Kannan.

Padma Subrahmanyam's dance style cannot be labelled "pure" by any stretch of the imagination. It might in all fairness be called eclectic for she takes movements and gestures from other Indian classical styles apart from Bharata Natyam. Also she uses some *karanas* (dance units) that fell into disuse generations ago. What she is able to do however is to make this eclecticism work on the stage and that, after all, is what matters in the end.

On December 13 Dr. Subrahmanyam gave a lecture-demonstration at the October Gallery where she explained some of her theories.

REGINALD MASSEY

37

Balasaraswati. <u>The Dancing Times</u>. LXXIV, 884, May 1984, p 681

Balasaraswati

BALASARASWATI, the great classical Indian dancer, died on February 9 in Madras at the age of 64 after a long illness. Srimati T. Balasaraswati was born Madras in 1919, and has been described as the most celebrated dancer of India, the last of the *devadasis*. Born into a family of dancers and musicians, her teachers were Kandappa, Gauri Ammal, Chinayya Naidu and Lakshmi Narayana Shastri. She performed in the West for the first time in 1961, and thereafter made many tours throughout Europe and the USA. She was resident teacher at Wesleyan University from 1962-1968, University of California at Los Angeles 1968, California Institute of the Arts 1972, and the Center for Asian Studies, University of Washington, Seattle 1968 and 1973. She received many awards in India, and in 1976 a full-length film on her artistry was directed by Satyajit Ray.

38

Indian Festival. The Dancing Times. LXXVIII, 925, Oct 1987, p 47

Indian Festival

by

REGINALD MASSEY

The photograph above of Nahid Siddiqui was taken by Mary Tisserand.

IT has been many years since one has seen so many dancers and dance styles from the Indian subcontinent here in London. Through a combination of fortuitous circumstances the great Kelucharan Mohapatra stopped over here en route to the States from the Soviet Union where he danced for the inauguration of the Festival of India. At the same time the innovative Chorus Theatre of Manipur were in London hotfoot, as it were, from the Edinburgh Festival. Mohapatra and the Manipuris were the stars of the season since they represented the most traditional elements, on the one hand, with the most intelligently experimental on the other. The programmes were spread over August and September and the main venue was The Place although Riverside Studios and the Bharatiya Vidya Bhavan were also involved.

Kelucharan Mohapatra, now in his seventies, comes from a long line of hereditary dancers and was himself a *gotipua*, a boy temple dancer. The *gotipuas* were the counterparts of the *maharis*, the female temple dancers, and had to leave the temple on attaining manhood. However, while in the temple they often wore women's clothes and danced women's parts. In *Kuru Yadhu Nandana* Mohapatra showed his mastery of female roles when he danced Radha, Krishna's beloved. She asks Krishna to prepare, dress and decorate her for the act of love; with yearning in her eyes she begs her lord to linger and be patient. Here was the erotic, quite explicit, which transcended desire and became a thing of pure beauty. And the miracle was achieved before our eyes by a balding man, not frail but far removed from the first hot flush of youth. In another memorable piece Mohapatra danced the famous Muslim poet Shala Beg who was stricken with leprosy. He opened in an attitude of *namaz*, prayer, and then acted out the valorous deeds of Krishna. At the end of his devotions the poet shows his ulcerous limbs to the god. He does not ask to be cured but the implication is clear: cannot the god who slew the powerful demon Hiranya slay the evil disease that afflicts the poet? Kumkum Mohanty, one of Mohapatra's leading pupils, partnered her master but her best piece was the solo dance that vividly expressed a maiden's love for Krishna. The musicians — Bhubaneshwar Misra, composer and violinist, Rakhal Chandra Mohanty, vocalist, and Rati Kantha Mohapatra, percussionist — were outstanding. This Odissi group appeared on September 4, 5 and 6 at The Place and one felt disappointed that their stay was so short.

The Chorus Theatre of Manipur was at Riverside Studios from August 25 to September 5 and then had a single night (September 10) at The Place. The brainchild of Ratan Thiyam, the dance theatre was established in 1976 with a view to fusing the old with the new. Not only are some of their themes relevant and modern but some even cross barriers of time and culture. Last year, for instance, they produced *Antigone* using Indian classical and traditional dance forms. Here they presented *Chakravyuha* which is based on an episode from the *Mahabharata* epic. The *chakravyuha* was the malevolent and all-consuming military machine which destroyed the young warrior Abhimanyu, the son of Arjuna. It is a dance drama of magnificent power and emotional grandeur with Abhimanyu eventually attaining heavenly bliss. Martial arts mingled with an eclectic dance idiom and resulted in a moving dance theatre production.

Lively Kathak was seen at The Place on September 2 when Nahid Siddiqui danced brilliantly. The *tarana* in the ten beat time cycle *jhaptal* was sparkling and the dancer's natural vivacity was evident throughout the evening. However, there was a dearth of expressive dance. The whole of the *après* interval consisted of *nritta* or pure dance. How one missed a good *thumri andaaz*, a poem sung and performed with interpretations at several levels through mime, gesture and *nigah*, expressive use of the eyes.

The Bharata Natyam at The Place was a mixed bag. Pushkala Gopal and Unnikrishnan (September 8 and 9) and Shobana Jeyasingh (September 11 and 12) started with an unfortunate disadvantage. The centrepiece for each of the four nights was the same subject matter by the selfsame writer, that is, the *Ramayana* of Swati Tirunal's rendering. Ms. Jeyasingh's task, however, was the more difficult as she danced solo with recorded music. Ms. Gopal had musicians from India and had a male partner as well. Nonetheless, a slim youngish Rama dancing with a matronly Sita seemed incongruous though Unnikrishnan's Kathakali item *Vanavarnana*, which detailed the adventures of the hero Bhima in a dense forest, was an example of what the dance drama from Kerala can offer.

Chitra Visweswaran's appearance at the Bharatiya Vidya Bhavan (September 5) was pure joy. Her *Padavarnam* — a very full account — was a rare combination of lyric beauty and controlled energy and in *Ariven Aiyya* she painted a true to life cameo of a jealous mistress. Ms. Visweswaran's Bharata Natyam flows from Thanjavur, Vazhuvur and Pandanallur. Her style might not be the favourite of the Kalakshetra academics but she has her own imprint and possesses what can only be called charisma. Hence she was in that select band of classical dancers chosen to represent India in the USSR. With her were K. Rajasekharan (conductor and vocalist), R. Visweswaran (vocalist), C. P. Arumugam (percussionist), A. V. Unnikrishnan (flutist), and Srikala Narasimhan (dancer).

39

Dance Study Supplement – Asian Dance. <u>The Dancing Times</u>. LXXX, 955, Apr 1990, pp i–viii

Dance Study Supplement
part seven

ASIAN DANCE
by
Reginald Massey

This month the Dancing Times Study Supplement looks at Asian dance.

Reginald Massey's involvement with Indian dance includes lecturing and criticism as well as contributing articles to Dancing Times for a number of years. He has written on music and dance for The Times, The Guardian and The Musical Times, as well as providing material for international reference books such as the Encyclopaedia of Dance and Ballet and Everyman's Encyclopaedia. Former editor of Asian Post International and An Indian Bookworm's Journal (published from London) he is currently Foreign Editor of Arabesque (published from New York). His books on Indian cultural subjects include the recently published The Dances of India.

When the term 'Asian' is used in Britain it is generally understood to be a person, thing, form or style pertaining to the subcontinent of South Asia. More particularly, it means Indian, Pakistani or Bangladeshi. 'Asian' also applies to Sri Lanka. This point has to be made from the start since, correctly speaking, the Chinese, Vietnamese, Japanese and all Russians east of the Urals are 'Asian' but are not known as such in Britain.

In this Supplement the term 'Indian' will be used since India is the largest country in South Asia both in area and population. 'India' will be used in a loose geographical sense (such as 'the subcontinent of India') rather than as a political entity.

40

ASIAN DANCE

BHARATA NATYAM	- Tanjore, Madurai, Madras, Belur
KATHAKALI	- Kerala
KATHAK	- Lucknow, Jaipur, Delhi
MANIPURI	- Manipur
ODISSI	- Orissa

Map showing the areas from where the main classical dances of the India-Pakistan sub-continent originated. Courtesy of Reginald Massey.

Anna Pavlova dances Radha to Uday Shankar's Krishna.

and on every festive occasion Punjabis will most surely dance the lively Bhangra. In recent years disco-Bhangra (a contemporary, western type of Bhangra) has become the rage with young British born Asians.

There can be no doubt that Indian classical dance — perhaps a better description would be 'art dance' — has evolved from and been nourished by the many traditional folk forms of the subcontinent. Because of the caste system art/classical dance was practised by families of dancers and the art was handed down from father to son or mother to daughter. Thus over the centuries the classical dance of India has been refined and enriched and has, as was bound to happen, accumulated a distinguished corpus of theory and tradition.

So seriously was dance taken that the *Natya Shastra*, a textbook on the performing arts, came to be revered as

Ram Gopal in his famous role as Shiva, the hunter. Photograph by Houston Rogers.

History and Background

The diversity of India is astounding. Indeed, the variety of India's ethnic types, religious beliefs, languages, dress, social customs, climate, food habits, and folk and classical art forms very often bewilders Indians themselves. The vast majority of the population is rural and life has changed comparatively little over the centuries. Dance is an integral part of Indian village life and there are various types of traditional and folk dance forms. These can, for example,

be identified as sacrificial, instructional, martial, talismanic, seasonal, celebratory, or devotional. There are also several forms of dance drama which use both religious and secular themes.

In Britain one is likely to see folk dances peculiar to the following regions: Bengal and Bangladesh, Gujarat, and Punjab. Bengali and Bangladeshi dances often mirror the life of the fisherfolk and paddy-growers. The community Garba dance and the stick dance (Dandiya Ras) might be seen at any Gujarati function,

holy writ. The book was compiled some time between the 2nd century BC and the 3rd century AD and its authorship is shrouded in antiquity. However, it is commonly believed that the book was written by a sage named Bharata. The *Natya Shastra* is a fascinating work for not only does it examine aspects of production but it also discusses the movements of the limbs, the representation of the sentiments, emotional states, style, and even the canons of criticism and assessment.

A subject as rich and complex as Indian dancing has several aspects. Just as the precisely cut facets of a rare diamond combine to reveal its myriad beauty so, with Indian dancing, its full beauty is revealed only when all its many aspects are united in perfect balance. In order, therefore, to be able to appreciate this balance, it is necessary to have some idea of its constituent parts.

Dance was classified as either *margi* or *desi*. That which was sacred to the gods and danced for them was *margi*, while the dance for the pleasure of humans was *desi*. It was further defined as either *tandav* or *lasya*.

Tandav was first danced by the god Shiva, Lord of the Dance, who then conveyed this art to mortals through his disciple Tandu. Shiva is the symbol of procreation and it is because of this that **tandav** is often regarded as a male dance. To assume this, however, is to limit its field. **Tandav** covers all dance which expresses actions and feelings with strength and vigour, whether it is danced by men or women. When it is danced without facial expression it is called **Prekashani tandav**, and when it includes facial expression it becomes **Bahurupa tandav**. There are seven generally accepted types of this **tandav** said to have been danced by Shiva:
Ananda, expressing joy.
Sandya, the evening tandav.

(Above) Ram Gopal and Alicia Markova practise hand gestures for a collaborative performance at London's Palace Theatre in 1960. Photograph by Jack Blake. (Below) Kathak dancers Uma Sharma and Devilal in Mughal costume. Photograph by Marc Alexander.

Uma, the **tandav** he danced with is consort Uma.
Gauri, the **tandav** he danced with his consort Gauri.
Kalika, which he danced when he slew the demon Kalika.
Tripura, which he danced when he slew the demon Tripura.
Samhara, his dance of death which symbolizes the release of the soul from the prison of Maya or illusion.

Lasya is that element of the dance which is graceful and delicate and expresses emotions on a gentle level. It is usually associated with the dance of women because Parvati, the consort of Shiva, taught it to Usha, the daughter of the sage Bana, who then passed on the art to the women of India. However, since love is the predominant sentiment in **lasya**, it is also danced by men when their dance expresses this sentiment. Krishna's dance with the *gopees* (milkmaids), for example, is in **lasya**.

There are three main components, *natya*, *nritta*, and *nritya* which, together with their subsidiaries, make up the classical dance.

Natya is the dramatic element of a stage performance. There are three main points of resemblance between **natya** and classical Greek drama. Bharata defines **natya** as 'a mimicry of the exploits of gods, *asuras* (demons), kings, as well as of householders of this world'. This is very similar to Aristotle's description of tragedy as 'an imitation of some action that is important, entire and of proper magnitude'. In both cases there

ASIAN DANCE

(Above) Raja and Radha Reddy, who have taken Kuchipudi (the style of Andhra Pradesh) to many countries. Photograph courtesy of the Bharatiya Vidya Bhavan. (Below) A karana demonstrated by Bharata Natyam dancer Swarnamukhi at the Bharatiya Vidya Bhavan, London. Photograph by Madan Arora.

is a purpose beyond pure entertainment. For the Greeks tragedy effected, 'through pity and terror, the correction and refinement of such passions'. The **Natya Shastra** maintains that drama will teach and, in addition, 'give courage, amusement, as well as counsel.' Aristotle's drama comprised fable, manners, diction, sentiments, music and decoration, postures, gestures, words, representation of temperaments and music.

Here the similarity ends, for to the Greeks tragedy was the highest form of drama, and tragedy in the Greek sense did not exist in Hindu drama.

In Greek drama the emphasis was on hearing, hence Aristotle was primarily concerned with the fable or plot and the poetry in which this would be expressed. For the Hindus, the impact

was mainly visual and so Bharata gives detailed attention to the manner of presentation.

Unlike Aristotle, Bharata does not forbid the representation of violent action on the stage, provided always that — however terrible — it is shown with control and beauty.

Hindu drama was not bound by the unities of either time or place quite as strictly as was Greek drama and its idea of unity of action too was somewhat different. The aim was rather, towards a general unity of impression.

Nritta is the rhythmic movement of the body in dance. It does not set out to express a mood or sentiment or tell a story and therefore uses no facial expression. It visualizes and reproduces music and rhythm by means of abstract gestures of the body and hands and by extensive and precise use of footwork.

Nritya is that element of the dance which 'suggests *ras* (sentiment) and *bhava* (mood)'. Both **ras** and **bhava** are conveyed through facial expressions and appropriate gestures.

Another important text is the *Abhinaya Darpanam*, ascribed to a theorist named Nandikeshvara who is thought to have lived in the 2nd century AD. Nandikeshvara concerns himself with sentiment and mood and how these are to be 'carried towards the spectators' by means of eye movements, facial expressions, and gestures of the body and hands.

Indian dancers recognize nine basic sentiments or emotional states: Love, Humour, Pathos, Anger, Heroism, Terror, Disgust, Wonder, and Serenity. There are, of course subdivisions of each. A mother's love for her child, for instance, is different from a man's love for his mistress. The training of a dancer, therefore, is expected to equip him or her to evoke the appropriate sentiment in the onlooker. To this end the *Natya Shastra* enumerates thirteen gestures for the head, thirty-six glances, seven movements for the eyeballs, nine for the eyelids and seven for the eyebrows. The nose, the cheeks, the lower lip, each have six gestures and the chin has seven. There are nine gestures for the neck. Sixty-seven hand gestures are listed. There are three movements for the belly, and five each for the chest, waist, sides, thighs, calves and feet. Besides these there are thirty-two movements for one foot and include the calf and thigh.

The four ideal postures of the body in movement are described as slightly bent, equally bent, greatly bent, and thrice bent.

A complete unit of dance includes the posture of the body in conjunction with hand and foot movements. There are 108 dance units in all, ana these are carved into the four gateways of the temple of Chidambaram in South India.

Every Indian dancer is made to memorize the following lines of Nandikeshvara:

Where the hand goes, there also should go the eyes,

Where the eyes go, there should
go the mind,
Where the mind goes *bhava*
(mood) should follow,
And where *bhava* goes, there *ras*
(sentiment) arises.

There are five main classical
dance styles in the Indian subcontinent.
For the sake of convenience we shall first
consider Dasi Attam which is native to
Tamil Nadu in South India. It derives its
name from its chief exponents till the
1930s. These were the *devadasis*, or
'women in the service of the gods' [see
Glossary]. Dasi Attam means 'the dance
of the devadasis' and the style was
practised within the temple precincts in
honour of the presiding deity. Relatively
recently the term Bharata Natyam has
come into general use for the dance
hitherto known as Dasi Attam. This
change was made in an attempt to
dissociate the art from the *devadasis* who
had come to be regarded as disreputable
practitioners with loose morals. Be that
as it may, it was the *devadasis* who kept
alive this beautiful and sculpturesque
dance style.

Kathakali, the powerful all-male
dance drama of the south west state of
Kerala, has an immediate and
unforgettable impact. The grand

(Above) The stick dance, Dandiya Ras, is a popular folk form with members of
the Gujarati community in Britain. Photograph courtesy of Reginald Massey.
(Below) Kathakali is the powerful dance drama from Kerala in South-west
India.

costumes, halo-like head dresses, and
symbolic make-up are all larger than life.
The content of the dance dramas is
usually taken from the great epics of India
and so Kathakali is about good and evil,
cosmic forces at work, and the bloody
battles of gods and demons. The dancers
were usually men of the Nayar caste, the
warriors of Kerala. Now, however, a few
non-Nayars have been allowed into the
professional companies.

The classical style of North India
and Pakistan is Kathak. Though its origins
are clearly Hindu, Kathak was adopted by
the Muslim rulers and became a
sophisticated court dance. The footwork
of Kathak is complex and the movements
are subtle and suggestive. The fast
pirouettes, complicated variations and
changing tempi create suspense that is
heightened with each successive
variation. The essential unity and rapport
between dancer and drummer is
maintained without a single lapse and
there is a final ecstatic catharsis that can
only be likened to a volcanic eruption.

The Manipuri dance had its
origins in north-eastern India. There in
the picturesque Manipur valley the local
people, the Meities, created a style that is
soft, lyrical, sensitive and gentle. The
Meities have an inherent love for the art
of dance. The kings of Manipur were
often accomplished dancers themselves
apart from being heads of the guild of
dancers, the *palaloisang*.

Orissa, in eastern India, has been
called the land of temples. It is the home
of the Odissi dance which is sometimes
also called Orissi. Dancing girls have
been dedicated for service in the temples
from very early times, but there is
evidence of an unbroken tradition of this

ASIAN DANCE

in Orissa from the 9th century AD. These girls, known as *maharis*, together with their male counterparts, the *gotipuas*, have preserved the art. Odissi is unique in the sense that though the dance movements are essentially south Indian, the accompanying music is north Indian. Also much use is made of the 'thrice bent' posture as well as slow, sensuous hip movements.

There are other classical styles that are still danced. Moreover, there has been in this century a movement towards experimentation and the creation of new eclectic styles. Two geniuses must be mentioned in this respect: the Nobel prize winning poet Rabindranath Tagore evolved what has come to be known as the Santiniketan style, and Uday Shankar — the elder brother of the musician Ravi Shankar — created the Uday Shankar style.

Today, although dancing has been firmly reinstated, **gurus** and dancers are faced with the task of extending and enlarging the classical repertoire to include subjects which will be relevant and meaningful to the last few years of the twentieth century. Blind orthodoxy endangers authenticity. The classics must, and always will, be a source of inspiration and instruction, but even these cannot come to life without being informed with the integrity of contemporary creative experience. Experiment and innovation are essential to the survival of a tradition. Bharata himself was aware of this and in our own century Tagore has written. 'There are no bounds to the depths or to the expansion of any art which, like dancing, is the expression of life's urge . . . Genius is defined in our language as the power that unfolds ever new possibilities in the revelation of beauty and truth . . . Greatness, in all its manifestations, has discontent for its guide . . .'

Asian Dance in Britain

If dance is the expression of a peculiar creative urge that is inherent in all types of human beings then all dance is essentially one. Forms, however, differ on account of a number of variables — be they physical, geographical, cultural, religious, or even economic. Pavlova was intensely aware of these varieties and it was she who discovered Uday Shankar in London in 1923. He was then an art student but Pavlova recognized his potential as a dancer-choreographer. She asked him to help her to choreograph *The Hindu Wedding* and *Radha and Krishna* and she danced Radha to Shankar's Krishna. Pavlova had earlier toured India and the Far East in search of dance material and had created *Ajanta Frescoes*, based on ancient Buddhist cave art near Bombay, which she danced at Covent Garden.

For a period Shankar was based in England where he rehearsed his company in the picturesque setting of Dartington Hall in Devon. His friends the Elmhirsts of Dartington Hall later generously financed Shankar to start his

(Above) Kathak dancers Pratap and Priya Pawar are among the best known Indian dancers living in Britain. Photograph by V K Verma. (Below) Bavaani Nanthabalam teaching Bharata Natyam gestures in a London Primary School. Photograph courtesy of the Academy of Indian Dance.

Prakash Yadagudde, Bharata Natyam teacher at London's Bharatiya Vidya Bhavan, corrects the arm positions of a young pupil. Photograph courtesy of the Bharatiya Vidya Bhavan.

well known dance centre at Almora in India.

Uday Shankar's Company of Hindu Dance and Music was greeted with accolades not only in Britain but also in France, Germany, Italy, Austria, Scandinavia, Switzerland and America. In 1938, Shankar returned to India.

The very next year, in 1939, Ram Gopal left India to tour abroad. Here was a dancing phenomenon who had been trained in the strictest classical schools of South India. He had been fortunate: two great dancers had taught him. Minakshisundaram Pillai was his Dasi Attam *guru* and his Kathakali *guru* was the legendary Kunju Kurup. In Britain Ram Gopal's purity of style made an immediate impression on discerning dance enthusiasts. It was Ram Gopal, wrote Cyril Beaumont, 'who, through his initial London recitals, opened our eyes to the varied styles and rich vocabulary of Indian dance.' His most celebrated presentations in Britain were *Dances of India, Legend of the Taj Mahal*, and *Dance of the Setting Sun.*

With London as his home Ram Gopal travelled the world expounding the dance of India and making 'converts' wherever he went. He still lives in London though he spends a lot of time in his beloved Venice.

Ram Gopal started a school of Indian dance in London where he taught and also brought over qualified teachers from India. Other pioneers were Ayana Deva Angadi and his writer-painter wife Patricia Angadi. Their Asian Music Circle will be fondly remembered. Angadi cajoled, pleaded, put in his own money and somehow managed to get first rate Indian dancers and musicians to perform in this country. Men like Ram Gopal and Angadi carried on for years on end without a penny from public sources

since in those days funding bodies — which were few and far between — would not countenance Indian dance.

However, Indian dance was not without friends. Pre-eminent among these was the Queen's cousin the Earl of Harewood. As head of the Edinburgh Festival he provided Indian dancers and musicians with the prestigious platform they deserved. Wider acceptance and recognition came when dance magazines — notably the *Dancing Times* — and the quality dailies began noticing Indian dance performances.

A few art conscious businessmen like Ramesh Patel have put money into Indian dance. Patel's *Nava Kala* group did tremendous work for aspiring young Asian dancers and musicians living in Britain as did Birmingham's Star Agencies, the National Association of Asian Youth and the numerous Indian associations in the various cities. The ferrying over and presentation of dancers from India has been undertaken by organizations such as the *Bharatiya Vidya Bhavan, Sanskritik, Nadabrahman,* the Academy of Performing Arts and Music, and *Utsav.* Today, however, there is a strong feeling among many dancers of Asian origin in the United Kingdom that funding from public sources should be used to train, encourage and promote British Asian talent. Many also believe that funding — scarce and insufficient in any case — must go to practitioners of Indian dance directly rather than a sizeable proportion of it being lost to them in administrative costs.

Naseem Khan's *The Arts Britain Ignores*, published in 1976, and the Minority Arts Advisory Service furthered the cause of Asian dance. Today Indian dance is actively promoted and taught by a number of organizations such as the *Bharatiya Vidya Bhavan,* the Academy of

Indian Dance, and *ADiTi*. However, the many dance teachers toiling away quietly at grassroots level — often in difficult circumstances — must not be forgotten. □

Bharata Natyam dancer Alarmel Valli. Photograph by Ray Clarke, courtesy of The Bharatya Vidya Bhavan.

Bharata Natyam dance students, from the Bharatiya Vidya Bhavan, in prize-winning choreography by their teacher Prakash Yadagudde which was seen on March 25 when London Weekend Television broadcast the winning entries of the 1990 LWT/ ILEA Arts Festival. Photograph courtesy of LWT.

Glossary
Terms used in Indian dance:

Abhinaya: expression
Adavu: dance unit (Bharata Natyam)
Amad: entry (Kathak)
Apsara: divine nymph
Arangeetram: debut of a dancer (South India)
Asura: demon

Bhajan: hymn
Bhava: mood
Boles: rhythmic dance syllables

Chaal: walk or gait (Kathak)
Chakkiyar: reciter of sacred texts in the temples of Kerala
Cholom: a masculine variety of dance (Manipuri)

Desi (dance): for the pleasure of humans
Devadasi: woman servant of the gods, temple dancer (Bharata Natyam)
Dupatta: veil, also called orhni

Gath: dance in which a story is told (Kathak)
Gharana: school or style
Ghungurus: ankle bells
Gopee: milkmaid, young woman

Hasta: hand gesture (Kathak)

Jati: complex rhythm pattern in footwork of Bharata Natyam

Kalasam: short piece of pure dance (Kathakali)
Karana: a unit of dance including poses and hand and foot movements
Keertan: devotional song
Kriti: dance-song

Lasya: feminine aspect of dance
Layakari: the dancer's mastery of the variations of rhythm within the time measure (Kathak)

Mahari: female temple dancer (Odissi)
Margi (dance): sacred to the gods
Mudra: hand gesture
Mukhabhinaya: facial expression

Nattuvanar: musician, dance master (South India)
Natya: the dramatic element
Nayaka: young man, hero
Nayaki: young woman, heroine
Nritta: pure dance
Nritya: the expression of sentiment and mood in dance

Pada: love lyric
Padam: that part of a Bharata Natyam performance where the padas are interpreted through abhinaya
Puja: service of devotion

Raga: musical mode, melody archetype
Ras: sentiment, emotional state, also dance

Sahitya: literature, literary content
Sakhi: confidante

Shishya: student, disciple
Shringar: love
Sloka: short religious verse
Sollukuttus: rhythmic dance syllables (Bharata Natyam)
Sum: the first and key beat of the time measure

Tal: time measure in dance or music
Tandav: masculine aspect of dance
Tatkar: footwork (Kathak)
Tirmana: a short brilliant succession of adavus (Bharata Natyam)

Vipralambha: separation in love

Selected Further Reading

All India, Reginald Massey (Editor), The Apple Press, London. 1986
Art of Indian Dancing, Projesh Banerjee, Sterling Publishers, New Delhi. 1985
Dance Dialects of India, Ragini Devi, Vikas, Delhi. 1972
Dance Dramas of India and the East, K. Bharatha Iyer, Taraporevala, Bombay. 1980
Dance in Thumri, Projesh Banerjee, Abhinav Publications, New Delhi. 1986
Kathak: Indian Classical Dance Art, Sunil Kothari, Abhinav Publications, New Delhi. 1988
Krishna Theatre in India, M. L. Varadapande, Abhinav Publications, New Delhi, 1982
Lesser Known Forms of Performing Arts of India, Durgadas Mukhopadhyay (Editor), Sterling Publishers, New Delhi. 1978
Religion and Theatre, M. L. Varadapande, Abhinav Publications, New Delhi. 1983
The Dances of India: A General Survey and Dancers' Guide, Reginald and Jamila Massey, Tricolour Books, London. 1989
The Encyclopaedia of Dance and Ballet, Mary Clarke and David Vaughan (Editors), Pitman, London. 1977
The Indian Experience, Ken Barrett and Suresh Sharma (Editors), Media Transasia-Thomson Press-Air India, Bangkok. 1982
The Splendours of Indian Dance, Mohan Khokar with photographs by Gurmeet Thukral, Himalayan Books, New Delhi. 1985
Traditions of Indian Classical Dance, Mohan Khokar, Books From India, London/Clarion Books, New Delhi. 1979
Traditions of Indian Folk Dance, Kapila Vatsyayan, Indian Book Company, New Delhi. 1976

Some useful addresses:

ACADEMY OF INDIAN DANCE,
16 Flaxman Terrace, London WC1 9AT
Tel: 01-387 0980

The Academy provides services to Indian dancers, operates a teaching programme through classes and schools' work, and organises workshops, lectures, etc.

ADITI,
(The National Organisation of South Asian Dancers)
Jacob's Well, Bradford, West Yorks BD1 5RW
Tel: (0274) 754090

ADiTi publishes a quarterly newsletter, and from May 1990 a Directory of South Asian Dancers, Musicians, Classes, Venues and Promoters.

BHARATIYA VIDYA BHAVAN,
(The Institute of Indian Culture)
4A Castletown Road, West Kensington, London W14 9HQ
Tel: 01-381 3086

The Institute teaches music, dance, drama and languages, and stages several art forms of India. The premises include a Library on Indian Culture, a Bookshop (also selling music cassettes and records), and a small theatre.

NATIONAL RESOURCE CENTRE FOR DANCE,
University of Surrey, Guildford, Surrey GU2 5XH
Tel: 0483 509316

Large resource centre for all forms of dance, not specifically Indian, but the NRCD has now produced a video tape of GCE 'A/S' level African and Indian studies.

SUSSEX VIDEO,
Microworld House, 2-6 Foscote Mews, London W9 2HH
Tel: 01 266 2202
Fax: 01 226 2314

Supplies tape/slide sets, video and audio tapes of Asian dance, music and culture produced by Indian film-maker Deben Bhattacharya.

Resource list part 4

Some outlets from where books on Indian dance are available:

BOOKS FROM INDIA,
45 Museum Street,
London WC1A 1LR

LOTUS MULTICULTURAL BOOKSHOP,
10 The Crescent,
Hyde Park Corner,
Leeds LS6 2NW

SANGAM BOOKS LTD.,
57 London Fruit Exchange,
Brushfield Street,
London E1 6EP

SHAKTI BOOKS,
46 High Street,
Southall,
Middlesex

SOMA BOOKS,
38 Kennington Lane,
London SE11

Indonesians and Indians. The Dancing Times. LXXXI, 961, Oct 1990, pp 37-38

Indonesians and Indians

The very close cultural ties between the sub-continent of India and the archipelago of over 13,000 islands (yes, thirteen thousand) that make up the Republic of Indonesia were demonstrated ably and beautifully during the successful *Island to Island* festival at London's South Bank Centre from July 28 to August 5. Over 60 performers from the Indonesian Arts Academy, led by their director Dr Sri Hastanto, came to Britain under the patronage of the Prince of Wales and charmed their audiences with delightful dancing, singing and gamelan music. Indeed, the QEH became an Indonesian island in London with educational programmes, workshops on gamelan playing, exhibitions of batik, and several informal performances. There was, also, a whole programme on Indonesian literature and — allied to the festival proper — an exhibition of manuscripts from Indonesia in the King's Library at the British Museum which will continue till October 29.

The dancers opened at the QEH with the specially commissioned ballet *Bima Suci* which dealt with the complex personality of the Indian warrior Bima who embarked on a quest for self-knowledge and the nectar of eternal life. Two characters ('white' Bima, danced by the choreographer of the ballet, I. Nyoman Cahya, and 'black' Bima, danced by Samsuri) symbolised the conflict in Bima's soul. After many agonies and 'dark nights of the soul' the opposing elements in the hero's psyche were reconciled through the divine intervention of Dewa Ruci (portrayed by a female dancer Hodowiyah Endah Utami).

Topeng Klana, a powerful mask dance, was brilliantly executed by Sunarno Purwolelono who depicted the anguish of a king insanely in love with a woman betrothed to another. The

Javanese Topeng, or mask dance.

sharp, sword-like manipulation of the dancer's red scarf was a clever device and told volumes. The techniques of Javanese theatre were employed in *Ganjur-Ganjret*, a piece which showed the antics of a pair of comic servants and the soft movements of seven women dancers in *Gambyong Pareanom* were reminiscent of the Manipuri dance of north-east India.

The *Jaranan* (hobby-horse dance) from cen-

tral Java represented the popular folk idiom still so very popular.

From July 29 to August 12 a Summer School of Indian Dance and Music was held at the Bharatiya Vidya Bhavan in London when a multi-cultural group of over 60 participants were coached by four tutors who came over from India at the Bhavan's invitation with the assistance of the Arts Council of Great Britain and Air India. Kumudini Lakhia, who once partnered Ram Gopal in London and who now runs a dance centre in Ahmedabad, conducted an intensive course in Kathak. Alarmel Valli from Madras taught Bharata Natyam. T. V. Gopalakrishnan, also from Madras, took classes in South Indian music and from Calcutta there was Nishat Khan (scion of an illustrious musical family) who coached in North Indian music.

I only had time to sit in on one of Kumudini Lakhia's classes for senior students, a number of whom are already professionals performing in public. The conviction I immediately arrived at was that every single penny spent on the summer school was well worth it.

REGINALD MASSEY

Indian dance in Britain

By Reginald Massey

The conundrums of cultural expression in a world that is fast approaching, if it isn't already, a global village are fascinating and worthy of serious attention. Moreover population movements on a scale and frequency not possible in earlier times have posed challenges, created at once problems and opportunities and increased the possibility for great success and dismal failure.

In Britain the presence of a significant number of citizens with origins in the Indian subcontinent has resulted in a lot of 'Asian' art in this country. However a few facts, not generally known or accepted, require statement. Many Asians here have come from Africa, the Caribbean and other outposts of the former British Empire and hence have had little or no direct contact with India for two or three generations. Those who came from the Indian subcontinent are now ageing. Their children and grandchildren are British born and it is they who are now in the majority. Quite naturally, their cultural conditioning, tastes, aspirations, and expectations are, by and large, the same as those of the rest of the British population of comparable age.

So when we talk specifically of 'Asian' dance in Britain, what are we talking about? I've heard scathing remarks that add up to: "there ain't no such thing". However, crowds of young British Asians regularly swarm into Bhangra dance halls in London, Birmingham, Leeds, Manchester and other cities. Their elders regard these Bhangra halls as dens of iniquity for the young of both sexes have the opportunity of mixing freely, a practise that runs counter to Asian tradition.

Nevertheless, the young continue to sway and swing to heady rhythms that, though peculiar to the Punjab, have assimilated rap, rock 'n' roll as well as other elements. A *tehmat*-clad Punjabi peasant would be bewildered by this British Asian version of his native Bhangra. In fact, he would grunt most emphatically: "This ain't no Bhangra!" and add a colourful Punjabi expletive or two for good measure. Be that as it may, this is the real stuff. If there is a native British Asian dance, it is this particular strain of Bhangra.

But let me come to art dance. In the days when Uday Shankar and Ram Gopal enthralled audiences in this country there were few Asians resident in Britain. Those Britons who went to see and lionize the two great dancers were educated, culturally aware, and belonged to the middle or upper classes. Today the situation is vastly different. The Britons who have discovered Indian art dance in recent years come from a variety of backgrounds. Some have had practical experience of ballet, others believe passionately in multiculturalism, and still others are escapees from what they feel is the stifling atmosphere of the British dance establishment.

Those Asians who have done well, or even reasonably well, in Britain now constitute a sizeable British Asian middle class. This middle class, in common with any other emergent middle class, is culturally self conscious. It is this class that desperately desires its next generation to be 'cultured'. Hence they want their children to be aware of Asian culture, a culture to which they themselves had no access since they were too busy trying to improve their economic lot. Although they have only a hazy and somewhat confused understanding of Asian culture, they nevertheless believe that it is something lofty and worthy of study. That notion, in itself, is a worthy one.

Where there is a demand, it is soon met. Several teachers of Indian classical dance and music are now busy in this country and there seems to be no shortage of bright, keen pupils.

Centre, Uday Shankar at the height of his career, a photograph taken in London when he was about age 50.

Left, Mrinalini Sarabhai another of the great dancers who performed here in the late 1940s and subsequently. Her daughter Mallika is also a well known dancer; Mrinalini now teaches, directs and choreographs at her dance centre in Ahmedabad.

Right, the young Ram Gopal dancing on the shore near Government House, Bombay, in 1944. Gopal's first London season was at the Aldwych Theatre in 1939, followed by numerous return visits with his own company of fine dancers.

49

This, at face value, is a good thing. However, in order to shed further light on the British Asian dance scene, let me report some relevant remarks made by Birju Maharaj whom I interviewed at length when he toured this country with a small group during October 1992. Birju Maharaj is the head of the Lucknow gharana, 'school/home', of the Kathak classical style of northern India. He hails from a distinguished dynasty of dancers and choreographers and apart from his adherence to the traditional codes of Kathak, has created Kathak ballets in an attempt to enlarge the appeal and scope of Kathak. With Birju Maharaj was his pupil and dance partner Saswati Sen who, on occasion, made a point or two.

The interview was conducted largely in Hindi:

RM: It's been some years now since you've visited Britain. You've danced in a number of cities and towns on this tour and you've met various dance groups and teachers. What impression have you formed of the state of Indian dance in this country?

BM: It is good to see so many people, both Asian and British, showing such an interest in Indian dance. Wherever we danced — whether in Birmingham or Aberdeen — we danced to packed houses. Perhaps this might have happened because it is not every year that a Kathak group led by a guru tours the United Kingdom. Anyway, we were feted by one and all. Indians, Pakistanis, Bangladeshis, Sri Lankans, and Asians from Malaysia and the West Indies came to see us dance.

RM: Did you meet any dancers and teachers?

BM: Yes, we saw a few.

RM: What did you think of them?

BM: We did not see every dancer/teacher of Indian dance in Britain. And, of course, all styles are taught here. So far as Kathak is concerned, two of my students are teaching here. Of the others, I cannot say, for neither did they fully learn from me nor were they full-time students at the Kathak Kendra.
(The Kathak Kendra in New Delhi is the leading school of Kathak dance in India and Birju Maharaj is the chief teacher there.)

RM: Would one be correct in saying that, by and large, the standard of Indian dance teachers here is satisfactory?

BM: From what I have heard from the gurus of other styles, I would say, yes. But we have also heard of a few cases of very poor teaching.

RM: There's good and bad everywhere, I suppose. I'm sure there must be some very bad teachers in India as well.

SS: True. But in India the bad ones are soon found out and find it difficult to attract students.

RM: What do you feel about the teaching of a classical dance on foreign soil in a completely different atmosphere?

BM: I strongly believe that all teachers and senior students must spend time in India regularly. There they should have intensive courses from the gurus of their respective styles. This is absolutely necessary. I have seen the classical style of my forefathers being slowly, but perceptibly, changed and even eroded. This is only natural, since the cold and the wet here causes rust!

RM: Would you, therefore, say that it is only natural that a foreign-born person cannot master Indian classical dance?

BM: Certainly not. I have had foreigners come to me in India and their hard work and dedication to our dance has been an inspiration to my Indian students. I can think of two or three foreign students of mine who turned out to be excellent Kathak dancers.

RM: could you name one?

BM: Yes, Veronique Azan. She is French but has lived in India for many years and is now married to an Indian. She is a most gifted Kathak dancer.

RM: Turning to another subject: let's talk

Birju Maharaj and Saswati Sen who toured the UK during October last year, sponsored by the London based Asian Music Circuit. In India they have just completed a TV series on the history of Kathak dance which has been scripted by Jiwan Pani and directed by A Chandra.

about your Kathak ballets. Why did you undertake to use Kathak, which is essentially a solo form, for the purposes of full-length ballets?

BM: Yes, now first of all let me stress that in no way am I in the business of watering down Kathak. Classical Kathak is, as you say, a solo art form and must remain so. That is what I dance and that is what I teach.

However, one must experiment. Hence my ballets.

In the old days, only those who wanted to take up dance as a profession went to the gurus and spent years with them, and eventually only a very few became first class professional dancers. Now, of course, the scene in India has changed. Students want to study dance as they would any other subject like, say, literature or economics. Others wish to learn dance, not to become professionals but out of sheer interest.

SS: Many girls, for example, learn dance in a very dedicated way just to enhance their social and cultural accomplishments. Many young men in India prefer their future wives to be good at music and dance.

BM: So, you see, we cannot ignore this vast reservoir of talent. We have to teach all those who wish to learn, otherwise we would be failing in our duty. Of course, those students whom we feel have the makings of professional dancers are put through a hard period of training.

But to come back to your question regarding Kathak ballets. These give us the opportunity of using large numbers of students with various talents. Each in his or her own way contributes to the whole work. It also teaches our students to work together constructively and builds up their self confidence.

RM: So you are in favour of experimentation and innovation?

BM: Yes. But I'm against those who do so for fake reasons.

RM: Fake reasons?

BM: Indeed. A number of dancers in this day and age try to make an impression. Or do strange experiments in order to raise grants and subsidies. They concoct odd parallels in the hope that they might be creating something new. This is happening in the West as well as in the East. I say experiment, but only after you have mastered the grammar of your own language. Would you start writing a book if you were unable to construct a simple sentence?

So many dancers today do not know enough of their own particular idiom. And yet they have the cheek to 'create' as they say, a new style! Such experiments are bound to end in failure.

RM: Thank you for being so forthright and thank you for your time.

After considering Birju Maharaj's various comments I have the following suggestion to put forward:

The time has now come when teachers of Indian dance and music in the United Kingdom should be required to have some kind of registration. After all, many of these teachers work in schools and colleges that are funded from the public purse. Therefore, only those qualified and registered with an independent and competent authority should be permitted to teach. This body, needless to state, will be composed of unbiased persons who have no personal or professional axe to grind and who are above art politics. Indeed, LEAs must insist on proper qualifications and registration before employing Indian music and dance teachers. It is thus that adequate teaching standards will be ensured.

Registration must only be granted to those who have satisfied a board of examiners in both theory and practical expertise. Such a course will not only safeguard the pay scales of bonafide teachers but will also raise their professional status. ∎

Note: Reginald Massey, lecturer and writer on Indian dance, has written for *The Times, The Guardian* and the *Musical Times*, as well as providing material for international reference books. Former Editor of *Asian Post International* and *An Indian Bookworm's Journal*, his recent work has included the book *The Dances of India* and the *Dancing Times* Study Supplement on Asian Dance.

50

Anandavalli. <u>The Dancing Times</u>. LXXXV, 1013, Feb 1995, pp 469-471

Anandavilli

By Reginald Massey

In September 1970, I saw Anandavalli dance in London and wrote the following in this magazine: "Judged by any standards, Anandavalli is a brilliant dancer. I cannot

Anandavilli photographed by Roy McAuley.

imagine what she will be like in five years' time." She was, I recollect, barely in her teens and was introduced by Ram Gopal at the V&A Museum Lecture Theatre. Since then Anandavalli has lived in Sri Lanka, the land of her birth; Singapore; and, since 1985, in Australia of which country she is now a citizen. Her dance centre Lingalayam flourishes in Sydney and she has attained a high reputation.

On December 17, I saw Anandavalli again in London, this time at the Bharatiya Vidya Bhavan in West Kensington and was thrilled beyond measure for here was a charismatic dancer whose every movement radiated what can only be described as artistic truth. Her theme, *Shiva-Shakthi*, the power that pervades the procreative process, was delineated through two different styles, namely, Bharata Natyam and Kuchipudi. The Bharata Natyam items were choreographed by Udupi Laxminarayan and the Kuchipudi pieces by Vempati Chinna Satyam, both leading *gurus* in their respective fields.

The evening's main offering personified four aspects of the supreme female principle: Meenakshi, the fish-eyed beauty; Kamakshi, the creator; Mahishasura Mardini, the destroyer of demons; and Parvathi, the divine consort of the god Shiva who dances in union with the male principle. Each was described in a typical situation which provided Anandavalli with ample scope to act and mime. Her expressive hands told volumes and her eyes illuminated subtle shades of meaning. Indeed, her *abhinaya*, ability to convey emotion, was superb. Also, her sense of rhythm — so clearly expressed through precise footwork — added to the pleasure of the individual dances.

The music, though taped, was first class and thoroughly satisfying. It is obvious that

Anandavalli's *gurus* in south India, to whom she regularly returns, have showered on her their choicest gifts.

Possessed of intelligence, beauty, energy and wit, Anandavalli is — I believe — well poised towards acquiring international status.

Please note that the name of the dancer was incorrectly spelt in the title of the original article. The correct spelling appears within the text and in the reference at the top of this page

Indian Dance Captivates. The Dancing Times. LXXXV, 1020 Sep 1995, pp 1161-1163

51

Indian Dance Captivates

A South Bank Festival and a Summer School

By Reginald Massey

London's eminence on the international dance scene was further reinforced in July when Jay Visva Deva's Sama Performing Arts Network presented an Indian festival at the Queen Elizabeth Hall. Three styles were richly represented: Kathak from northern India (July 18); Bharata Natyam from southern India (July 28); and Odissi from eastern India (July 29).

Birju Maharaj, hereditary Kathak *guru* of the Lucknow school, was in fine form — having recently triumphed at the Avignon Festival — as was his chief pupil and partner Saswati Sen. The *Invocation to the Trinity* was a suitably serious piece without trace of fake religiosity and this was followed by Saswati Sen's exhilarating solo in *teental*, the popular time-cycle of 16 beats. Birju Maharaj then sang, quite marvellously, an enchanting hymn by the mystic poetess Mira which was interpreted in terms of dance by Saswati Sen.

The Kathak *guru* is possessed of immense charm and charisma and explained in his inimitable fashion (in a colourful mix of English and Hindi) that he wanted to present Kathak in a *mehfil* milieu, that is, in the atmosphere of civilized informality that had developed in the sophisticated court of Avadh where his ancestors had flourished under royal patronage. He demonstrated the vast range of

Kelucharan Mahapatra, master of the Odissi style, specialises in feminine roles. Photograph by Avinash Pasricha.

Bharata Natyam specialist Alarmel Valli in an item depicting a disconsolate woman.

the Kathak *boles*, mnemonic syllables, first recited by him and then taken up by the percussionist on the *tabla*, pair of drums. There then followed *jugal-bandhi*, friendly competition between dancer and *tabla* player, and snappy sessions of *savaal-javaab*, 'question-answer'. However, Birju Maharaj's *jugal-bandhi* with the veteran Kishan Maharaj (*guru* of the Benaras school of the *tabla*) could not catch fire though it went well enough. This was not because either was wanting in any way: but a *tabla* maestro who is a solo star in his own right is hardly the best choice for the role of accompanist.

After the interval the magic of Kathak came into its own when Ambika Prasad Mishra, Birju Maharaj's regular percussionist, rejoined the musicians. So infectious was the *mehfil* ambience and so enthusiastic the audience participation that Birju Maharaj might have danced the night away. But the programme was already well beyond its scheduled limit, and time and the Tube have scant respect for art.

Alarmel Valli, well known as a Bharata Natyam exponent, was trained by leading teachers of the Pandanallur school which

emphasizes clarity and intensity. Over the years she has performed at several world dance festivals and is therefore conscious of the parameters and exigencies of western urban life. Her programme, therefore, was 'structured' in a western sense which many, though not all, Indians would fine 'irksome' and 'restrictive'. Without making value judgments of any kind whatsoever, the point must be made (and I believe it is a significant one) that the approach to art in east and west is different.

In terms of Bharata Natyam, however, Alarmel Valli's dancing was satisfying. Her *varnam* explored the love that is both physical and spiritual, the ecstasy experienced by mystic women of both east and west. And her delightful portrayal of the young woman who has fallen hopelessly in love with the dashing youth who used to pester her when they were children rang true to life's little ironies.

The legend of Krishna's enchanting music was encapsulated in *Kavadi Chindu* and the success of the piece was due, in no small measure, to T.R. Moorthy's flute playing. Also, Prema Ramamoorthy's vocalisation was faultless.

52

Kelucharan Mahapatra, leading *guru* of the Odissi style, is a respected figure. When young he was a *gotipua*, male temple dancer, in Orissa and hence his psyche is tinctured with religious fervour. He is a rare dancer and it was a thoroughly good idea for Madhavi Mudgal to get her teacher to accompany her to London. *Yahi Madhava*, the only item that Kelucharan Mahapatra performed, is taken from Jayadeva's *Gita Govinda*, a 12th century classic. He danced both Krishna, who in this piece is disgustingly unfaithful, and Radha the woman who pines for Krishna and whose heart aches when she discovers his cheating.

Kelucharan Mahapatra's acting evoked the deepest emotions and was an example of what has been called the willing suspension of disbelief. The dancer-actor is an old man; the audience hardly noticed, and if some did, the fact was irrelevant. What we saw was a young woman; hurt, anguished, distraught. We were on her side; for her lover, though a god, was wayward, inconstant. Like the Greek gods, Krishna too was overfond of the daughters of men. His excuses were lame, Radha rejected them and so did we.

Madhavi Mudgal is a worthy disciple of her great master. Her *Pallavi*, a flowering, as it were, of musical motifs in movement, was excellent and her portrayal of the woman waiting for her lover — who never came — was touching. The last dance, *Sohamasmi* ('I am That'), was on the subject of all-pervading reality and the essential unity that binds the cosmos. It was cleverly choreographed and danced beautifully by Madhavi Mudgal, Bindu Juneja and Rekha Tandon. The vocalist, Madhup Mudgal, was excellent throughout.

The one item that disappointed was *Siva*

Above, Guru Birju Maharaj in Mughal costume. Photograph by Marcus Massey.

Below, Odissi dancer Madhavi Mudgal. Photograph by Avinash Pasricha

Tandava Stotra, which portrayed the god Shiva and his consort Parvati. The essential, endearing aspect of Odissi is its flowing, feminine quality but the subject matter required a virile, powerful dance idiom; hence the dichotomy. It is pertinent to mention here that Orissa's great Jagannath temple at Puri is Vaishnavite, not Shaivite. Dedicated to the god Vishnu, it was chiefly in this temple that the Odissi dance developed and attained distinction.

The Bharatiya Vidya Bhavan, the Institute of Indian Culture, in West Kensington held its annual summer school of music and dance from July 23 to August 13. Saswati Sen took classes at master, advanced and intermediate level in Kathak while, likewise, Udupi Laxminarayan, the celebrated *guru* from Madras, taught Bharata Natyam. The school was well attended by United Kingdom students with a sprinkling from across the Channel as well.

Saswati Sen's solo programme on August 5 was a veritable *tour de force*. Her items were well chosen and included pure, expressive and powerfully dramatic pieces. Her *layakari*, fast tempo rhythmic variations, and pirouettes were breathtaking. *Bhaya* ('Fear') had her own choreography with music composed by Birju Maharaj. Set in today's urban environment, the dance was an example of what can be achieved through careful and considered innovation by a vastly talented dancer who has mastered the grammar of her art. She ended with an unusual item depicting the god Rama, a subject not often touched upon. The vocalist was Guru T.V. Gopalakrishnan, from Madras, who is versatile in both north and south Indian music. ■

Darpana Delights and Excites. The Dancing Times. LXXXVI, 1022, Nov 1995, pp 147-149

53

Darpana Delights and Excites
The Vision of Mrinalini Sarabhai

By Reginald Massey

The Darpana Academy of Performing Arts which flourishes in Ahmedabad, capital of the Indian state of Gujarat, was founded by the visionary dancer-choreographer Mrinalini Sarabhai in 1949 who is not afraid to use what she finds worthwhile and stimulating from any corner of the earth. The academy's new amphitheatre, Natarani, opened last December and has become, characteristically, a venue for experimental work not only from different parts of India but for foreign productions as well.

Over the past half-century Sarabhai has grown from strength to strength and therefore one must speak of her before focusing on the British tour that she and her company undertook recently (October 6-November 4). Born into a distinguished South Indian family, she broke with tradition and decided to learn Dasi Attam, the dance of the *devadasis* or temple courtesans. Later, however, in order to make Dasi Attam respectable and hence acceptable the middle classes labelled it Bharata Natyam. Sarabhai studied the austere and disciplined Pandanallur style and was soon recognised as a rising star. Indeed, she was briefly associated with Ram Gopal when he was based in Bangalore.

Sarabhai's background was one of civilised protest much influenced by British radicalism during the inter-war period. It was the time when educated Indians read the *New Statesman* studiously, courted arrest for demonstrating against British rule and, when in jail, were permitted by their British jail superintendents to research and write books against British imperialism. Nehru, for example, would never have become a major writer had it not been for British jails. It was cricket, played out in a decent sort of way, when batsmen did not wait for umpires' decisions but walked. Gandhi encapsulated the India-Britain situation when he explained that the crusade was not against Britons or Britain but against imperialism and exploitation. Sarabhai's sister Lakshmi, however, did go a step further: she joined the ill-fated Indian National Army that resorted to armed conflict.

Sarabhai's time at Shantiniketan with the Nobel prize winning poet Tagore, in the period just before the sage died in 1941, was a turning point in her life. She discovered, due in no small measure to Tagore's prompting and encouragement, her vocation which was to experiment with the art of dance. Her marriage to the eminent scientist Vikram Sarabhai, member of a wealthy industrial family, was a marriage of true minds. They were a formidable duo; she moved to his home city, Ahmedabad, and Darpana came into being. To her academy she invited leading *gurus* and embarked upon a training programme whereby she imparted dance

Two studies of Mrinalini Sarabhai — "she is still a star". Photographs by Eric Richmond.

education to literally thousands of students.

In her inaugural talk at London's Nehru Centre on October 6, Sarabhai dwelt upon the crucial difference between how the *gurus* taught her and how teaching is conducted at Darpana. "My teachers said do this or do that, and I was expected to obey commands. What intrigued me was: *why* this and *why* that? At Darpana discipline is far from lax but we allow our students to ask questions. That is the great difference." She is, in the western sense of the term, one of India's first, and foremost, choreographers and her imprint was evident on the whole repertoire which was brilliantly conceived consisting, as it did, of classical, creative and folk components.

The main performances in London were for a week at the Bloomsbury Theatre where, on October 9, Mallika (Sarabhai's daughter and best known for her leading role in Peter Brook's *Mahabharata*) opened with a brilliant

display of classical Bharata Natyam and Kuchipudi, both South Indian styles. *Kauthuvam*, a danced prayer, invoked the blessings of the gods on the proceedings and the *Varnam* took the form of a lament by a maiden who had fallen hopelessly in love with Kartikeya, son of Shiva and god of war. The arrows of Manmada, the South Indian Cupid, had pierced her heart and left her distraught. The expressive dancing made it quite clear that in matters of love it is the woman who, in the end, comes off worst.

Kuchipudi, originally performed by young men of the priestly caste, was danced with verve and, in *Lakshmi Vilasam*, Mallika very adroitly used a 'male' style to underline a 'female' point, namely, that the god Vishnu and his ten incarnations (best known among them being Rama and Krishna) were victorious through war and conquest whereas Lakshmi (Vishnu's consort) and her incarnations won over human hearts through love and compassion. Lakshmi is always depicted as standing on a lotus flower (like Aphrodite she emerged from the deep waters) and, appropriately, Mallika drew the picture of a lotus with her feet while dancing the final stages of the item.

In *Lakshmi Vilasam* it is Lakshmi who distracts the demons with her beauty while the gods make off with the *amrit*, nectar. However, in the 'authorized version' of the myth it is the alluring Mohini who does the deed.

A few years ago in *Dancing Times* I wrote about *Shakti: the power of women*, a dance creation by Mallika and John Martin of the London-based Pan Project. I was therefore looking forward to seeing the British premiere of *Sita's Daughters*, their latest collaboration. I was not disappointed. It is an uncommon, powerful, moving piece; a one-woman dance theatre which uses most skilfully music, movement, masks and language. Martin's direction is tight, compelling; and Mallika had many in the audience reaching for their handkerchiefs.

Sita's Daughters tells of man's inhumanity to woman and targets ancient tradition, modern hypocrisy and today's widespread macho attitudes. Although it centres on India (some of the episodes are based on actual events) the call to women, and to men as well, is universal. The writing, by Manohar Aashi and Suniti Namjoshi, is at once pointed and ironic and although there is an unmistakable 'message' one never feels that this is a piece of feminist propaganda. In short, the writers, the director and the dancer-actress have achieved the magic that we call art.

By absolute chance, the staging of *Sita's Daughters* on October 12 coincided with *Karwachoth*, the day when Hindu women fast and pray for the health and longevity of their

husbands. A laudable exercise, no doubt;
however, there is no day set aside for men to
undertake similar abstinences for their wives.

Sita's Daughters made me angry on
many scores, not the least of them being that it
was put on for only one night on the London
stage. It has also incensed fundamentalists and
rightwingers in India, but for different reasons.
Hence the death threats to Mallika. Mr
Rushdie is not alone.

Mrinalini Sarabhai's *Memory is a ragged
fragment of eternity* was another moving
piece. It was choreographed in 1963 as a
protest against women's suicides on account
of the brutality meted out to them by husbands
and in-laws. The use of Bharata Natyam to
address contemporary problems was novel in
the early 'sixties and since then Sarabhai has
gone on to greater experimentation. However,
it was good to see her dance again after a long
time. She is still a star.

Tagore had just completed his famous
dance-drama *Chandalika* when Sarabhai went
to study at Shantiniketan. Much to her surprise
he cast her in the title role and since then she
has herself produced *Chandalika* several
times. It tells of an outcast girl who offers
water to a thirsty Buddhist monk. He thanks
her gently; indeed, is the first man ever to
have treated her with respect. She falls in love
with him, but she is an Untouchable and he a
holy man vowed to celibacy and poverty.
Tagore castigated the caste system which was,
and still is, the curse of Hindu society.

In this latest production of *Chandalika*
(on October 14) Mallika danced the girl,
Bharat Baria was the monk and Sarabhai
portrayed the mother who, out of love for her
daughter, cast a spell to ensnare the monk. It
was all there: passion, pathos, sorrow,
compassion and, above all, conflict.

Janavak, which was started in 1982, is the
folk and tribal dance arm of Darpana. It is
doing wonderful work in terms of research
and performance and is much in demand at
international folk festivals. Janavak presented
many examples of folk dance from the
different regions of India and also conducted
workshops in London and at other venues
while on national tour.

Also, among the creative pieces mention
must be made of *Shadows*, choreographed by
Sarabhai, and Mallika's *Ceremony One, Mean
Streets on Earth, Thattukazhi* and *Jazz Tillana*
which had music by Trilok Gurtu and Daniel
Goyone.

Sarabhai gave a number of lectures and
taught master classes at the Bharatiya Vidya
Bhavan in West Kensington. The musicians,
led by Maheshwari Nagarajan, were brilliant
throughout. ■

In Praise of the Pioneers

First published in *South Asian Dance – the British experience*. <u>Choreography and Dance</u>. Vol 4, Part III, 1996, Harwood Academic Publishers

Indian dance, music and art are now, as it were, widely 'accepted' in Britain. Local education authorities and arts bodies allocate funding for Indian dance, several teachers earn a living teaching dance and many cultural organisations hold regular classes and workshops in London and other cities. Moreover, the interest is not confined to Asians alone; many young, and some not so young, people from non-Asian backgrounds are learning Indian dance with great interest and enthusiasm.

Now all this has not happened overnight and must never be taken for granted by those who practise Indian dance in Britain either professionally or as a part-time activity. It has been a difficult, uphill struggle covering a period of several decades and many have dedicated their lives to the cause of propagating Indian dance in this country. It is in their honour that I set down this record of achievement.

However, first things first. The British ruled India and, as has always happened, the norms of the rulers were imposed upon those who were ruled. The British cannot be blamed for this phenomenon for they themselves experienced the same process under Roman occupation. When Britain was part of the Roman Empire the majesty of Roman law was brought to bear on the natives and Latin became the language of learning and culture. It was the Romanized Britons who occupied the positions of power when the legions departed and, quite naturally, the Roman practices continued. Nevertheless, because of the Roman conquest, Britain became, in effect, a 'civilized' country. Before the Romans came the British tribes were clad in fur and woad; by the time they left many Britons were clad in cloth. Indeed, some might well have been clad in cottons from India for the Roman Empire was, history informs us, an important market for Indian textiles.

The British, who in Victorian times were governed and guided by the severe Protestant ethic, took the business of the 'White Man's Burden' very seriously. Only a century ago most Britons, and the English in particular, righteously believed that it was their God-given duty to 'civilize' the world. *Pax Romana* had been replaced by *Pax Britannica*.

Roads and railways were constructed in India. British law was enforced. *Thuggee* and *sati* were stamped out. The English language was made paramount. European medicine replaced the Ayurvedic and Unani systems. In education, Shakespeare and Shelley took over from Kalidasa and Jayadeva. The list is endless. All that was British was unquestionably the best and, by implication, all that was Indian was bad, inferior, corrupt. It is, therefore, not surprising that

when the British saw erotic sculptures adorning temples and *devadasis* plying their trade within the temple precincts, they condemned Hinduism and all its works. It is a fact that in 1927 in Madras Presidency alone, which was part of British India, there were 200,000 temple prostitutes. Mahatma Gandhi was so disgusted with the situation that he wrote:

> There are, I am sorry to say, many temples in our midst in this country which are no better than brothels.
>
> *The Harijan*

Apart from a few British administrators such as Sir William Jones, who founded the Asiatic Society of Bengal in 1784, most had no time for any Indian art. The exotic Hindu temple dance of South India was something that the average European could not comprehend. Hence it was ignored. The active opposition came from upper-caste 'enlightened' Hindus who were clearly embarrassed by what was happening in the temples. They could not see that it was the *devadasis* who had kept alive a great dance art.

Dasi Attam, the classical dance of the *devadasis* which had been handed down from mother to daughter for many generations, was not something that decent, educated Indians discussed in the presence of their children. High caste Hindus would certainly not allow their daughters to have anything to do with a dance art that was practised by prostitutes. But, thankfully, there are always exceptions to the rule and, as often happens, the poets were the exceptions. In 1901, the Bengali poet Tagore founded Santiniketan with, it is germane to mention, assistance from the English educationist Leonard Elmhirst who had founded Dartington Hall in Devon. Tagore emphasized the importance of music, dance, drama, painting and sculpture in the process of education and got leading musicians, dancers and artists to teach at Santiniketan. Later, in 1930, the Kerala poet Vallathol established the Kerala Kala Mandalam to fulfil his dream of reinstating the Kathakali dance drama to its former glory. Such was Vallathol's persistence that when he could not raise funds from the usual sources he set up a lottery, cajoled and persuaded his many friends and admirers to buy tickets and with the profits started his dance school.

In the province of Madras the stigma of temple prostitution continued for a long time and it was only when two Brahmins, E Krishna Iyer and Rukmini Devi, started their dance crusade that *Dasi Attam* became 'respectable'. In the process *Dasi Attam* was rechristened *Bharata Natyam*. I use the word "rechristened" advisedly. For rather like the early Christians baptising the pagan festivals and making them 'respectable', the Brahmin establishment of South India in the early decades of this century Brahminized the *Dasi Attam* into *Bharata Natyam*. What's in a name? a Shakespeare character queried and went on to suggest that it made no difference. But it does. Names are symbolic and in India surnames do not exist: traditionally, caste names serve as surnames.

57

When Indian dance had to struggle for recognition and identity in India itself, my readers can well imagine the position in Britain during the period before the Second World War. The dance scene, as a whole, was not as vibrant and varied as it now is even though Ninette de Valois had founded the Royal Ballet School in 1931 and the Royal Academy of Dancing had been going since 1920. It is worth recalling that classical ballet grew and was nurtured in Italy, France and Russia and it was only the dedication of Ninette de Valois, Marie Rambert, Frederick Ashton, Alicia Markova, Margot Fonteyn and other stalwarts that eventually put British ballet on the dance map of the world. British dancers, choreographers and dance enthusiasts were too engrossed with their own problems to be concerned about foreign forms and traditions.

There were, however, a few western dancers (incidentally, none of them British) who were captivated by Indian dance. During the early years of this century the American Ruth St Denis toured the world with her 'Oriental' *Radha Dance* and when she and her husband Ted Shawn started their famous dance centre at Jacob's Pillow they always welcomed Indian dancers there. Martha Graham, who trained at Jacob's Pillow, had the highest regard for India's dance culture, and the exotic Mata Hari toured far and wide with her 'Oriental' temple dances. Inspired by the Krishna legend, Fokine and Cocteau created *Le Dieu Bleu* in which the god was danced by Nijinsky and Karsavina was Radha.

In the twenties the great Pavlova toured India and the Far East. In Madras her Indian hosts informed her that Indian dance had all but died out and what was left was not worth watching. But, ever a searcher, she persevered and visited temples where the *devadasis* still danced. It was Pavlova who advised Rukmini Devi to give up studying Russian ballet and to rediscover the dance heritage of her own country. Thus, Rukmini Devi became the first and most significant dancer of South India who was not a *devadasi*. She founded the Kalakshetra Academy which has produced many of India's foremost dancers, and in her personal life broke with tradition and married an Englishman. Pavlova also inspired Menaka to become the first famous Kathak dancer who was not a *bai* or *tavaif* (courtesan). Before Menaka no decent Hindu, Muslim or Sikh family would have anything to do with Kathak. Kathak, it was widely believed, belonged to the *kothas*, whore houses.

The Shankar family were art conscious and even though Shankar senior was a lawyer and former minister in the state of Jhalawar, he often produced and directed plays. The family was a product of what has come to be called the Indian Renaissance. It started in Bengal, ironically, under the influence of the new liberal British education system which introduced upper caste Bengalis to the heady ideas propagated by free-thinking poets such as Byron and Shelley. The first Indian 'intellectuals', in the European sense of the word, were upper caste Bengali Hindus. This fact had far reaching implications especially when, I must point out, the

majority of Bengalis in pre-partition united Bengal were Muslims. Even today, more Muslims speak Bengali than do Hindus.

As a progressive Bengali Brahmin, Shankar senior encouraged his son Uday to fulfil his ambition which was to become a painter; and so Uday was sent to study at the Royal College of Art in London under Sir William Rothenstein. But the gods had other plans.

In 1924, Shankar senior was in London and organised a stage show for charity. He asked his son to help out with some dancing, which Uday did quite willingly. Pavlova, also then in London, came to the show and was so impressed by the young student's talent that she asked him to join her in the production of two short ballets on Indian themes that she was keen to produce. *The Hindu Wedding* and *Radha and Krishna* were significant landmarks not only because they gave Uday Shankar his first experience as a professional dancer (he danced Krishna to Pavlova's Radha) but also because he gained an understanding of the technical aspects of ballet production from a *guru* of Pavlova's stature.

Shankar was with Pavlova for a year and a half and then launched out on his own in Paris. In 1929 he returned to India, studied *Bharata Natyam* and *Kathakali* in the south, sketched the temple dance sculptures and friezes, and filmed many folk dances. He collected an accomplished group of dancers and musicians – which he called the Uday Shankar Company of Hindu Dancers and Musicians – and embarked for Europe. The whole Shankar family was involved in this self-financed and privately sponsored cultural enterprise. Uday Shankar's mother and his three younger brothers Rajendra, Debendra and Ravi were part and parcel of the company. The very thought of such an undertaking, even today, leaves one breathless. But then genius is akin to madness.

Uday Shankar was driven by destiny; wherever the company appeared it was crowned with stupendous success. For many years Shankar was based in England in the picturesque setting of Dartington Hall and it was from here that he and his company made forays far and wide. It was chiefly on account of Uday Shankar that India's dance and music gained world-wide respect and particularly so in Britain.

Ravi Shankar, the youngest of the Shankar brothers, who first appeared on the stage as a dancer in his brother's productions, has written:

> It is a rare thing for a person with no formal training to become a great dancer and a
> pioneer in the art as well ... He appeared, really, like a god, filled with an immense power
> and overwhelming beauty. To me, he was a superman.
>
> *My Music, My Life*

59

And I wrote the following in the London *Times* dated September 29, 1977:

> In the history of dance he will be remembered for the professional standards he set for
> Indian ballet, and for evolving a new style ... Shankar nurtured a galaxy of talent which, in
> later years, profoundly influenced the performing arts of his country ... More recently,
> however, he was criticised by the orthodox purists for having the audacity to innovate and
> fashion was in their favour. He died largely disillusioned but a lord of dance nonetheless.

The other genius to bring Indian dance to Britain and the West was Ram Gopal. He, moreover, had been trained and honed by *gurus* such as *Kathakali's* Kunju Kurup and *Bharata Natyam's* Meenakshi Sundaram Pillai and was a major dancer in India. He first toured abroad with the American *danseuse* La Meri and later, on his own, he took America by storm. In 1939, his London début at the Aldwych Theatre heralded a meteoric career in this country. He was invited to meet Queen Mary, leading figures of the world of ballet became his friends and, in 1948, Nijinsky himself came to see him dance at the Saville Theatre.

Ram Gopal had the charisma to influence people and to turn their hearts and minds towards things Indian. Markova danced Radha to his Krishna and there was a time when his name was synonymous with that of Indian classical dance. However, Ram Gopal was also very cosmopolitan: he lived well and he lived in style. In the sixties, I worked with him for a short while and had the opportunity of studying him at close quarters. His luxury flat in Chelsea was adorned with the most tasteful art from both East and West and he was visited by leading writers, poets, painters, film directors, actors and musicians.

For me, Ram Gopal proved that dancers transcend race, style and technique. To use his words, theirs is a "universal language of the body in any rhythm of the dance, be it Eastern or Western." (*Rhythm in the Heavens*). Of course, his background has much to do with his catholic views. His father was a cultivated Rajput from North India, his mother a Burmese lady of great beauty, and he was brought up in South India. As a boy, he first danced in a palace in Mysore. His cultural roots are thus rich and varied.

Over the years, Ram Gopal has worked ceaselessly for the cause of Indian dance, not only in Britain which he made his home but in India as well. A living legend of the dance, Ram Gopal now winters in his beloved Venice by the Grand Canal. Diaghilev lies on an island near Venice and I remember that I was taken by Ram Gopal on a motorboat to visit the island. Ram Gopal laid flowers on Diaghilev's grave with tears in his eyes. This is the first time that I have recounted this incident. I do so now because I fervently and urgently plead that Ram Gopal be honoured by both India and Britain for his services to the art of dance.

60

The writings and reviews of specialists such as Arnold Haskell and my friend the late Fernau Hall created an atmosphere of acceptance and understanding in this country. I would be failing in my duty if I did not record their contribution towards the present status of Indian dance in Britain. Also, *The Arts that Britain Ignores*, an incisive report by Naseem Khan, made educational and funding bodies aware of their responsibility towards a number of 'ethnic' art forms including Indian dance.

As a *Dancing Times* critic for the last 30 years, I must pay tribute to my editor Mary Clarke. She has always encouraged appreciation and objective appraisal of Indian dance and dancers.